A Little Bit Up

Writing has been a faint dream for Ian Stanley-Eyles since his days in High School. A sometimes blogger, and administrator for several Facebook groups and pages, he is expanding his passion into writing again. He has over a decade in volunteering, emergency services and public safety, demonstrating a strong interest in health and community. He currently runs an independent first aid training business in Victoria, Australia. With this, his first book, Ian begins to combine the two backgrounds into an intriguing tale of real people on a real trek.

A Little Bit Up
Meandering in Nepal
by
Ian Stanley-Eyles

INK Publications
Sebastopol, Victoria, Australia

Cover Design: © Katherine Smyth 2012
Cover and Internal Images: © Margaret Evans, Mike Evans,
Sandra Gormley, Ian Stanley-Eyles, and Kim Stanley-Eyles 2009

First Published by INK Publications 2012

PO Box 239, Sebastopol, Victoria, Australia 3356

©Ian Stanley-Eyles 2012

National Library of Australia Cataloguing-in-Publication entry

Author: Stanley-Eyles, Ian.

Title: A little bit up : meandering in Nepal / by Ian Stanley-Eyles.

ISBN: 978-0-9874304-0-3 (pbk.)

ISBN: 978-0-9874304-3-4 (ebook)

Subjects: Stanley-Eyles, Ian--Travel.

        Hiking--Nepal--Guidebooks.

        Nepal--Description and travel.

        Nepal--Guidebooks.

Dewey Number: 915.49604

Dedication

For my lovely Kim, my best friend, travelling buddy, partner, lover, and wife.

Introduction

"I wish you a very good journey to an unknown you've never seen." - Pieter V Admiraal

How does one start an introduction and not sound like a million other books? There is no easy way, so I will just begin by saying I hope that you gain an interest in travel, to push yourself outside your comfort zone and see the world for the wonderful place that it is.

This book grew from the journal entries, blog updates, five hours of video recordings and the more than two and a half thousand images collected during several trips to Nepal; first as travellers on a trek and later to obtain greater details regarding a health project.

One of the amazing things about trekking in Nepal is that every time you crest a rise or turn behind a bluff, a brand new vista awaits to delight the eye. Away from the teeming cities, the air is clear and fresh. The sounds are of nature and it is possible to go for a week or more without hearing machines. There is a joy in waking each morning to peaks rising thousands of metres above. Among the many locals we found an open friendliness and a happiness that can only come from those not encumbered with the modern life.

During this journey, I think I discovered more about myself in those few weeks than in the previous 40-odd years of my life. Now at the ripe old age of 44, I have a better understanding of who I am and where I fit into the greater scheme of things on this little blue planet.

My thanks go out to Mike and Margaret Evans for placing the challenge before me; to Sandra Gormley as a traveling companion and showing me that there is no reason to just sit on my backside; my darling wife Kim who journeys by my side every day of our lives together and kicked my bum all the way around the Annapurna Conservation Reserve. With his guiding light, gentle humour and determination that our trip be the biggest success, I say to Dorje Tamang thank you for showing us your country and telling of the needs of your home village. It is for you, saathi, your brother Dhanraj whom we referred to as Dhan, mother Chyoki and father Ngima, and all the villagers of Pattale that this book has been written. A portion of the profits from this book will go via the Pattale Health Trust Inc. in Australia to the Pattale Community Health Centre in eastern Nepal.

For her efforts in editing and keeping me on the straight and narrow, I thank my mate, author and part-time editor extraordinaire Kate Smyth from the bottom of my heart. To my proof reader, Jen Smith, thank you for weeding out the wheat from the chaff in this book. To the members of the Thorung Five, your valuable insight and additions made this a much more rounded publication. Particular mention should go to Kim, Margaret and Sandra for the extra editing and recollections that have helped to build a more complete picture.

A special thank you goes out to my reviewers Cameron, Caroline, Dani, Eva, Graeme, Ian, Janice, Kate, Katrina, and Tanya.

Please enjoy the read and Namaskar to you all.

Ian

Dereel 2012

Chapter 1 - Genesis

"For my part, I travel not to go anywhere, but to go. I travel for travel's sake. The great affair is to move." – Robert Louis Stevenson

It was in December of 2007 at a Christmas BBQ for my work colleagues that Kim got a phone call with an offer we had to seriously consider. At the time, she was working for Victoria's Country Fire Authority (CFA). Our friend Mike Evans, a wildfire instructor with the CFA, was arranging another of his trips to Nepal. Kim had been attending a staff Professional Development Weekend in Anglesea some time earlier where one of the presentations in personal development had been given by Mike about his previous journey to the remarkable country. It inspired Kim and she came home full of the wonder of the images she had seen. Mike was calling expressions of interest for another trip. The next one would be a trek around the Annapurna Ranges. He wanted to know if we would be interested.

Here we were being given the chance of going on an adventure; to be explorers. We would be explorers of a new personal horizon. It was exciting and daunting all at the same time. We both accepted that this might all turn out to be a pipe dream; that we would not get a chance to go. I honestly thought we would end up on the reserve list with dozens of hopeful candidates vying to be the ones to make it across the oceans and ascend the heights.

There was a fair amount of soul searching at the time as we both knew our fitness wasn't the best. I was worried about a family history of cardiac issues although doctors would not check me over "until you have chest pain." When I was 24 I had been diagnosed with Ankylosing Spondylitis (AS) which had been slowly destroying the cartilage in my spine and hips. At that point, the right hip was replaced. At the age of 26, the second hip was given a prosthesis too. Due to the artificial hips, my life had been sedentary, particularly desk work, for decades and within the previous couple of years a spur had begun to grow in my shoulder limiting its movement. To put it mildly, I was not trekking material. Kim had grown up on a farm in South-Western Victoria and had the 'country girl' wide shouldered frame. But doing facilitation and community education with the CFA, and being often office-based, she realised she was also wide in other places as well. But there was time to prepare since the trip would be in late 2009. We had a year and a half in which to get ourselves ready.

With that on our mind, we agreed that we would put in an expression of interest. We would put our hand up. Bluff and bravado won out. We could talk the talk and it was safe. After all, chances are we would only be on the reserve list. What likelihood would there be that we actually get to go? Nepal can be really popular with the emergency services in Victoria. Heaps of people would be falling over themselves to head out on this trip. But we were game anyway.

In early July 2008, Kim got the call that both excited and filled us with dread. Mike rang to say that we were in as a lot of people had not been able to commit to the journey. In fourteen months we would be winging our way across a fair swag of Asia to walk one of the greatest hiking trails in the world; the Annapurna Circuit.

On July 17th 2008, a get together was held at the rural home of Mike and Margaret Evans. It was there that we met some of Mike and Margaret's previous traveling companions, a future companion Sandra Gormley who had never been to Nepal before, and our guide. Mike had already been to Nepal in 2005, 2007 and 2008. Margaret had been in 2005 and 2007.

The shy, retiring young man, standing by the fire and enjoying some Australian beer was Nabaraj 'Dorje' Tamang. Standing somewhere around 5' 5" (165 centimetres) and weighing in at a slight 50-55kg, nevertheless he carried with him an air of quiet self-confidence and moved with the economy of motion only seen in the Nepali people.

A map was laid on the table with our proposed path pencilled in already. A typed version of the itinerary sat beside it. On the map it looked to be a fairly straight forward walk. In the background, footage from Mike and Margaret's previous trek played prophetically. Dorje took us through the essentials of the diet we would face, fitness required, purchasing of essential supplies, currency, accommodation, pack weights, health and medications etc.

The food was going to be purchased from a string of tea houses along the way. It would be simple but nourishing. However, since tea houses have limited cooking facilities, it was recommended that we plan what we would eat as it was faster to make a large batch of one dish rather than making five or six different meals. This a tough lesson learnt from the experiences of previous trekkers.

While a moderately fit person would be capable of walking the trail, it was recommended that we start a serious exercise regime as there was going to be quite a bit of climbing. It is important to point out that while Nepal is a small country, it consists of lots of up. In words it is difficult to explain but suffice to say there is 'Aussie up' and then there is 'Nepali up.' There are very few places that compare in terms of terrain in Australia. The term 'Nepali up' can mean anything from 20 degrees to 45 or more degrees of angle and these may go on for several hours of climbing. It would become clear that cardio training would be very important during the trip.

Some of our equipment we would need to get in Australia long before we left. Trekking boots were the most important. They needed to be broken in long before we boarded the plane. Certain items of clothing were essential to bring from home to ensure they were well constructed but other items we would procure from the numerous trekking supply shops in the Kathmandu tourist suburb of Thamel. We could easily have fitted out our packs almost exclusively from Thamel but more on that later.

Money was an important matter. Since the currency is still paper based, it has the potential for being forged. Exchanges in Kathmandu are well equipped to deal with world currencies but it is illegal to bring in Nepali currency from outside the country. The same goes for Indian 500 and 1,000 rupee notes. We elected to take Australian and a small amount of American currency with us. Dorje had a contact that would arrange the exchange and get us a good deal on the rate.

Accommodation while in the capital was going to be at the Benchen Vihar Guesthouse in the grounds of the Benchen Phuntsok Dargyeling (BPD) Monastery in the suburb of Chhauni. Once on the trail, it would be no problem locating guesthouses and tea houses where we could sleep for the night. The rates would be the equivalent of a few dollars per night. We were to discover that sometimes they were quite luxurious and on one occasion quite hideous. Since we would be traveling prior to the start of the official trekking season, pre-booking would not be required. While our itinerary gave us a good plan of where we would be staying, we were likely to be passing through villages perhaps once per hour. If we were running behind schedule, it would not be difficult to find a place to rest our weary feet.

There is a practice, even carried on to this day, of unscrupulous trekking companies heavily overloading their porters with weights up to 100kg. This is considered unethical and leads to a high rate of injuries amongst the porter workforce. While insurance is now compulsory when employing porters, it does not adequately compensate a family if the only provider of income becomes permanently injured. It was recommended that we maintain pack weight of between 15 and 18 kg. The porters would supplement the weight with their personal belongings.

Since health support is limited outside of the major cities, it was recommended that we visit our doctor to obtain the appropriate immunisations. Given the locations we were visiting, this consisted of the Hepatitis (Hep) A, Hepatitis B and Typhoid shots. Since Kim and I are Ambulance First Responders for Ambulance Victoria, we already had Hep B injections. I had paid for my own and included the Hep A injection at the same time. Hygiene maintenance would be essential to avoid illness whilst trekking. Small bottles of alcohol-based gels (or 'goo' as we came to refer to it) would become our best friends, to be used at every opportunity. It would ensure that none of us would suffer the indignity of belly troubles during our journey.

Be that as it may, we still had to consider what would happen to us should someone become ill. We also had to plan for the potential issue of Altitude Sickness or worse. Sandra had brought her own medications from home. Fortunately we would be able to buy a range of medications including antibiotics, constipation and diarrhoea tablets and Acetazolamide for altitude sickness from medication supply shops in Thamel. Enough tablets for the ten of us including porters and guide would come to around $AU20.00. It should be understood that there are concerns some medications could be counterfeit when purchased from these stores. Careful note should be taken of the labelling. One indicator of a product that is not legitimate is misspelled printing on the wrappers or boxes.

The next matter to be discussed related to our donations to the people of Nepal. It had become tradition that people joining these treks would find something that they could donate somewhere along the trail. This might take the form of cash for a specific project, books or pens for the local school, or even medical supplies. Since I was, at that stage, working for Ambulance Victoria First Aid as an instructor, we decided that perhaps medical or first aid supplies would be appropriate. We asked Dorje what his thoughts were. What would be the most useful items we could try and source? As expected, he talked about bandages and the like, but he also mentioned the need for safety razor blades. These were to be used for cutting the umbilical cords.

Hospitals can potentially be days away so childbirth is still performed at home. Razor blades are the most efficient way of cutting the cord. Kim and I decided to have a think about this to see if we could come up with a better way of achieving the same result and hopefully limit the wastage. We were to discover on arrival that there is no effective waste disposal or recycling program although the government is attempting to remedy this. Most people will dump their rubbish in the streets or into nearby rivers. Medical waste is not exempt from the same lack of regard for health or environment. It was not until a return visit in 2011 that I was to learn of attempts to dispose of medical waste by burning.

With some lovely food on board and having met both our traveling companions and our guide, we went our separate ways to prepare.

By the end of July 2009, we were training almost daily. It was not unusual for Kim to be able to watch an entire two hour movie on the DVD player while using the cross-trainer machine. My fitness level wasn't that far behind hers although I was to learn very quickly on the trek that I could have done much more. The hours on the cross-trainer certainly did us good and our metabolisms really began to fire. Our weight was already dropping while our heart rates were much lower than when we had started. My initial misgivings about my ability to complete the trip were now gone; not to return until we were well into the journey when physically and emotionally I was at my lowest point.

I had taken to hassling anyone I could think of at head office for advice and medical information. By the time of departure, I had a current copy of the Remote Area Nurse (RAN) Protocol manual for 2009 and an Emergency Management Australia (EMA) manual for medical services in disaster areas. In addition to some valuable advice from Group Manager Tony Oxford and RAN program coordinator Jenny Geer ASM, I now had a working knowledge regarding the approved method of sterilisation of medical equipment for when an autoclave or chemicals are not available.

By mid-August, we had met together for our final trekking group meeting and nutted out flight details and final information. With some gentle negotiation, first aid supply bundle materials had been bought or donated from work and a generous donation of nearly fifty umbilical cord clamps had been received from Unomedical in New South Wales. Each bundle was packed into a bag, purged of as much air as possible then heat sealed. By the time I was done, 12 bags of supplies were ready to fit into my bag.

There was so much left over that we would need to arrange for someone heading over again to take more at a later date.

Initially I had hoped my brother Peter might join us but circumstances did not allow him to make it. However he had some good advice based on his travels into the wilds of Australia. One thing he suggested was contacting the rural media to see if anyone was interested in doing a human interest piece. Sadly we didn't think of this until we were about to depart. On the morning of September 4th, I sent out a couple of emails, most of which have not been answered to this day. However within ten minutes, I received a phone call from the delightful Prue Bentley, a producer at ABC Ballarat, asking if I would be interested in having a chat with the morning show presenter, Steve Martin. Completely thrown by actually receiving interest, I threw together a few notes about the trip and what we were going to do with the first aid bundles. Twenty minutes later, with my limited knowledge of Nepal, I was live on radio chatting about our trip. Steve was a delightful host and I tried to give him as much information to work with as possible.

Not long after I had finished the interview, and having run to turn off the recorder that was sitting by the radio, Prue rang back and asked if we could try and keep in touch. I wasn't sure how it would work given the fact that the time difference is four and a quarter hours behind Australia. Apparently she did try and ring my mobile on a couple of occasions but was unable to get through. We did have some big mobile black spots on the trail, however the daily blog I was running did get quite a bit of use and I gather they may have referred to it once or twice.

That chilly afternoon we were ferried to Melbourne International Airport to meet our midnight flight by our friends Kate and Jen. A full moon was already rising in the clear brown-red sky of twilight. Stopping by my parents for a goodbye meal, we arrived at the airport where we arranged to meet up with Mike, Margaret and Sandra for the adventure of a lifetime.

The staff at Singapore Airlines were brilliant and even enquired if our bags needed to be marked as fragile because of the first aid supplies. While we said no, they did ensure that our bags were carefully packed and easy to get off the plane upon arrival. I took the opportunity to grab some emergency cash in US dollars from one of the money exchange companies at the airport.

I have a ritual about travel these days. Before I even hit the terminal, my pockets are empty; glasses, wallet and watch in my day pack. Clothing is the lightweight trekking type attire with no need for heavy belts. My trekking boots are only laced half way ready to be removed and I always pat myself down before approaching any security checkpoint or departure lounge. The reason is very simple. I know that the metal detectors are going to go crazy. I have two artificial hips after all. Where Ian goes, the alarms will follow. These days, Kim and I try to get a chuckle out of it. What we can't change about the journey is the fact that the detector will go off, so good naturedly I make my way through the arch and straight to the security staff for the regulation hand scan, pat down and questioning. More often than not, I will usually get the detection scan for drugs and explosives too. After the standard joke about whether the device will remove the lint or cat fur from my clothing, it's over to collecting my possessions and getting dressed again.

Kim finds this a continuing source of amusement that she doesn't think will ever grow old. One year in Queensland, she was practically rolling on the floor as the security attendant tried to get me to strip off in public to prove I had implants.

As for my hips, my current surgeon nearly had kittens when I told him where I was going for my holiday. After ordering a series of x-rays and comparing them against shots taken before and after the original operations, he was happy enough to send me on my way. His verdict was that after 17+ years, I was lucky to only have about two millimetres of wear on the original right side replacement. I really do owe him a photo of me on the Thorung La pass at 5,416 metres.

Nevertheless boarding was quick and efficient, our flight departed smack bang on time.

Chapter 2 - Inbound

"A good traveller has no fixed plans and is not intent on arriving." - Lao Tzu (570-490 BC)

For someone who had never been overseas before 2009, Kim was on a roll. Already we had been to New Zealand earlier in the year. Now there we were on the biggest flight of our lives that would take us right into Asia. Gee! Economy class had come a long way. Each seat had its own entertainment system with literally dozens of films and television programs on instant recall. When I first flew, it was one screen at the front of the section and a movie projector half way down the cabin. (Yes I am THAT old.) If you didn't like the movie, tough!

Meals were a darn sight better than my initial experiences on planes too. Since it was an Asian airline, the choice was either western or Asian but both were delicious. Irrespective of the fact that, only hours earlier, we had eaten with my parents I chose the chicken dish with the large dried red chilli on top. It was delicious. Before you say anything, yes airline fare can actually be edible.

I remember having a sleepless night. I was too wound up so spent a fair swag of the trip flicking from one movie to the next. Kim, with her innate ability to sleep anywhere, was out like a light and very comfortable. I think I dozed at times during the night but was awake again long before breakfast.

Since we had booked in after Mike, Margaret and Sandra, we were in a completely different part of the aircraft. We wouldn't catch up with them until we arrived in Singapore.

Swinging in over Sumatra in the pre-dawn dark, we touched down in Singapore at about 05:45 local time. Joining the throng of exhausted passengers, we disembarked and passed through the brief period of hot, humid air before entering the cool terminal. Interestingly, while some travellers headed for the toilets, many of them actually diverted to the "Smoking Room." Packed in like sardines, the air quickly became clouded with the dozens of cigarettes; the negative air pressure inside the room preventing any smoke from escaping.

We met up with the other three just inside the terminal building. With eyes hanging out of our heads, we made our way onto the robotic train that took us to Terminal 2. Here we just had to wait until the 09:05 flight to Kathmandu. Mike managed to stake out a patch of carpet at the departure gate and lay down for a long nap.

Kim and I spent time checking out this wondrous airport. From the windows, we could look across the tarmac to the deep storm water trenches used to collect the tropical rains. In the distance as the early morning light increased, the city could be seen coming to life. The thick, humid air was making it difficult to pick out fine details in the distance.

The various shops in the terminal deal in a multitude of the more widely used currencies at the same time. Credit card machines make the exchange conversion on the spot so whether you buy duty free or a cup of coffee, you know exactly what you paid in your home currency.

At certain major intersections, there are magnificent orchid gardens with koi ponds. Near one such garden, Kim made friends with members of a disabled table tennis team from Yemen. They needed someone to take their photos. Being the kind of person she is, Kim obliged and even posed in a few shots with them.

A butterfly house is open during daylight hours. Movie theatres operate for those who are on layovers for extended periods of time. Massage vendors as well as coin operated chairs in different parts of the terminal buildings cater for the weary traveller. There are free internet computers everywhere as well as a free wireless network.

Beside all of the travelators, large murals depicting elements of Singaporean culture gave a teaser to the tourists as they arrived.

The only drawback I found when we arrived at Changi was that I could not remember my phone PIN and the battery on the laptop went dead. So I beat a path to the free internet terminals and sent an email to Kate and Jen who were house-sitting. With some clear instructions, they were able to locate my PIN and email me. Wow, they were awake and answering emails. That was fortunate. With their efforts, a short while later I had the phone unlocked and I was ready for action. It even found a network in Singapore I could use. The problem then became that I couldn't make or receive calls. What the? Another hurried email to the girls set off a separate chain of events in Australia that would take a couple of days to resolve. Apparently my phone provider had rescinded my international roaming without notice. After some threats, I eventually began receiving text messages from the girls. They had bullied the operator into reinstating my access. They even pointed out to the 'helpful' operator that no, I could not ring the standard phone number in Australia for assistance as I was OVERSEAS with a phone I could not dial out on. To my lifesavers, I salute you.

Changi International Airport is one of those transit points dotted across the world where people stop over before changing planes for their final destination. Four terminals were built between 1991 and 2008 with a one-day record of 146,000 passengers passing through. And you can tell it has been designed as such. Hallways are wide and clear of major obstructions with separate aisles down each side for seating and the ever present travelator down the middle. Toilet facilities are spacious with regular attendants to ensure everything is kept spotlessly clean. A veritable army of cleaners are constantly trawling the hallways. Carpets appear to be cleaned every day. If they are not being washed, they are being vacuumed. It's a relatively quiet and hassle-free environment.

Having downed a coffee and sitting bleary-eyed, we were eventually called for our flight to Kathmandu.

Boarding the next flight from Singapore to Nepal, I struck the same problem. 'Beeeep!' "Here we go again," I said as I walked towards the beckoning security staff. In the background, did I spot the explosives detector device being warmed up?

Alain de Botton, in his book "*The Art of Travel*", remarks that we will write about point A and point B but we forget to mention the journey between the two. That might be because the journey is remarkably bland. I wanted to remember as many details of this journey as possible and to share them with you, the reader.

I could certainly rabbit on about the four plus hours of travel from Singapore to Nepal, the one short, well used video tape that looped on the overhead monitors ad infinitum, or the lack of radio channels. Kim head down in her copy of Lonely Planet's "*Nepal*," Margaret and Sandra snoozing the morning away, or the various half heard private conversations around me but that would be boring and I wouldn't buy a book like that either.

Below us passed Malaysia, Myanmar (Burma), Bangladesh and India. The coastal waters were sparkling in the morning sun. Assorted fishing and cargo vessels could be seen hugging the coast lines.

The terrain of the Kathmandu valley as we came in to land grabbed our attention. Like some giant hand had grabbed a tablecloth and scrunched it up, so did the landscape passing below and above us reflect the difficult and steep land upon which these lovely people live. Bright brown-orange scars passed by our windows where recently landslips have torn away the young skin of this country. Angry marks on the hills delineated where man has ripped away the clothing of trees.

The closer to the ground we descended, the greater the number of half finished, concrete buildings peeking out from the wildly overgrown shrubs, bushes and grasses. Half-finished as if saying to the casual observer, "If I am not complete, I pay no taxes on this." Or perhaps the precursor of the future needs for household growth.

Kim and I stared excitedly out of the window as the plane came in to land on the three kilometre long concrete runway at Tribhuvan International Airport. The airport fire station shot past our windows with all its fire appliances on display to the world. Tall, lush grasses grew almost to the runway border where a vain attempt was made to keep it cut. This must be a daily task since everything grows almost as you watch it.

Pulling up with nearly no turning circle remaining, the jet swung left toward the terminal building past a large UN helicopter, the whitewashed fuselage gleaming in the sun. We taxied past the formal gates of the VIP arrivals building. The palatial grounds were guarded by several khaki-clad soldiers in the full power of the noonday sun. Easing past the air force base, our Airbus edged towards its designated parking area.

We finally pulled up amongst other aircraft from nations across the world. Gathering our possessions, the forward door cracked open and the oppressive heat and humidity assailed us. Armed with the video camera already rolling, I tried to get in front of the others to film them coming down the stairs. Never did I think that I might be violating some security law not that any of the airline staff seem to actually care.

The weird thing was that we were loaded into a large, seat-less transit bus and driven in a big loop back to the dark brown, brick terminal building; A structure that was perhaps 150 metres from our aircraft. For some reason, we had to drive to the doors rather than walk such a short distance. Frankly, after that many hours on an aircraft, I would have been happy for the walk.

For some reason, I was surprised by the heat and humidity. After all, the capital sits at over 1,300 metres above sea level. It should be mild but hot, wet wind blows up from India and is turned, driven across Nepal by the majestic Himalaya. Tropical is the best way to describe Kathmandu. The whole valley is caught in the grip of monsoon season right up until September so temperatures above 30 degrees Celsius with humidity about 65% and rain fall reaching towards a metre should have been no surprise at all.

The relative cool and dark of the arrivals corridor was comforting. I caught a few brief minutes on the video camera before discretion got the better of me and I put it away in my day pack. Timing is everything. As we moved towards immigration, we encountered armed men in camouflage gear and knowledgeable men in white coats. It was the era of the outbreak of H5N1 or 'bird flu.' Every passenger was being scanned by an infrared thermometer. People failing the test were grabbed by the men in camouflage gear and bundled out of the hallway.

Feeling somewhat guilty that we had passed the test, we shuffled in to the immigration hall. This cavernous, low ceilinged room gave the impression that it had been built in the 1960s and nobody thought it would need updating. The floors were a well-used form of pale industrial lino tiles. All of the pillars cased in dark timber carved with intricate designs. Walls were painted either a beige or pale lemon although I can't remember exactly which. To our right, barricaded and unoccupied was a duty free shop. In front of us, were an official money changer and a purveyor of passport photos for those who chose to buy their visa in country rather than from the various missions around the world. In Australia, the cost of a visa is double what you would pay at Tribhuvan.

Grabbing the almost see-through paper visa application form from a small counter, we began completing the requested details. These were double checked by Mike before we trooped up the multiple queues attempting to arrange entry into Nepal. We joined the hopefuls with our requisite $US40 cash for our 30-day visa. On the walls, precious flat panel televisions showed various advertisements and tourism ideas. The staff were quiet and efficient but did not exchange pleasantries with the arrivals. Eventually our turns came and in a short matter of time, we were through. Our passports were duly stamped and our dollars receipted.

The next stop was the baggage collection hall. Here we found an area as big as the immigration area but looking more like a half empty factory from the 1960s; the carved timber pillars incongruous with the grubby 'lino' flooring. Staff hovered ready to provide assistance, for a suitable fee of course. Mike had this situation well in hand since it is illegal for staff to solicit money for work they are already being paid to perform. Combining his height and broad shoulders with a deep and firm "No," the staff would quickly withdraw. Their hands firmly planted in the pockets of their uniform pants; pockets that were supposed to have been removed months previously. We wrestled our own trolley and loaded our own bags, heading for baggage checking. In front of us was a trolley laden with cardboard boxes. The customs men decided that they were worth an inspection and we were not, so we ended up going straight through to the exit doors. Here spruikers for various hotels and tour companies vied for our attention. One of them was trying to get Kim's attention despite our protestations that we were being met and had accommodation. Through the exit doors, throngs of men searched for work from the newly arrived travellers; either driving or loading.

Amongst the sea of faces, one familiar grin could be seen. Accompanied by shy helpers, was Dorje. He immediately took charge of our trolleys and vociferously argued that he was responsible for the bags and the other locals could presumably take a proverbial 'jump.' As always, Dorje had a vehicle to fit everyone on board. The police objected to our loitering for the 'hellos' so we were moved along in that impersonal but polite way of police forces across the world.

Our bags were handed to the driver who deftly placed them on the roof of the mini-van. With our possessions now stowed, we climbed aboard the van and settled into our seats for the ride of our lives. Oddly no straps were used to secure the load nor seatbelts to secure us. One desperate man had run up and helped pass a bag to our driver. He then became insistent about being paid. Mike took pity and handed the man an $AU5 note. The man scampered off with his prize. The five dollars he had extorted considerably more than he deserved for lifting one bag. Mike claimed that it was the smallest he had.

So edging our way towards the exit signs, we prepared to face this foreign place called Kathmandu.

Chapter 3 - On the ground in Nepal

"The first condition of understanding a foreign country is to smell it." – Rudyard Kipling

The first thing you will notice about Nepal in September is the heat and humidity. The first thing assailing you about Kathmandu is the smell. The combination of rich vegetation, exhaust fumes, soil, rotting rubbish and freshly ground spices; a distinctly Kathmandu odour. Thick, dark green grass grew right up to the footpaths but was regularly mown. Lush, tall trees and shrubs in assorted shades of dark green grew tightly together behind the fences.

Our minivan passed down the access road from Tribhuvan International Airport toward Ring Road. We passed the police checkpoint searching vehicles entering the airport grounds. Surrounding us such strong, verdant growth spread out and up. At the juncture of the two roads, Sandra, Kim and I encountered our first Nepali traffic.

From our observation point in the rear seat of the minivan, we could see the chaos that is everyday driving in this nation's capital. Motorbike, bicycles, cars, vans, trucks, buses, 'tuk tuks', and even rotary hoes converted into a form of tractor jostled for precious space on the road.

Eventually finding a gap in the traffic, our driver turned right and joined the stream of traffic, pedestrians and cattle. Surreptitiously it seemed

Margaret was watching us out of the corner of her eye; a smile possibly hovering on her lips. It appears that first-time visitors to Nepal all wear the same stunned expression as they enter the traffic flow.

Roads are often noisy and crowded. Lanes are generally defined by the majority of traffic flow in any one direction. Turning lanes, if you can call them that, appear at will. Pedestrians take their life in their own hands navigating the vehicles. Stray dogs do the same. Motorbikes and overloaded bicycles weave amongst the moving and stationary trucks, cars, taxis, minivans, and cows. Every vehicle must dodge the assorted potholes. All around is a cacophony of horns.

The use of indicators appeared to be minimal on the roads. Often vehicles would change position with the tootle of horns warning other drivers of their actions. Buses and trucks have someone hanging out of the side of the vehicle to signal their intended direction of travel. As Kim said, "...I thought at one stage the van had bent in half' in its effort to squeeze through. Trucks attempted to compete with each other for the most interesting horn sounds. We greatly enjoyed listening for the different variations. The few traffic lights we saw on that first journey appeared to have been generally ignored whilst traffic police made an almost vain attempt to bring order to organised chaos.

Many of the cars are taxis since the cost of fuel is so high. That is, of course, assuming the locals actually have any fuel to procure. Those too poor to own a car may have a bike. Despite their size though, we saw quite a few bikes loaded to the gunnels with objects too large to be normally considered. On that first journey we watched a pushbike rider with eight or more lengths of metal navigating the traffic.

But despite the constant impending sense of disaster that should have pervaded the mass of activity in front of us, what we noticed was a surprisingly subtle spatial awareness between all the drivers, riders, walkers and cattle. In fact the traffic seemed to flow effortlessly. During those first few days we never saw any vehicle collisions. Dorje told me later that the most common vehicle fatalities in Kathmandu were usually late at night when the roads were clear and alcohol was often involved.

Despite the fact we were on Ring Road, which in theory should take us around to our destination very quickly, the mass of traffic made it almost impossible to go any direction faster than walking pace. The side of the road was lined with brightly painted trucks, some of which spilled onto the road itself. Drivers would be forced to navigate around the obstructions. Idle workers could be seen sleeping on top of loads of bricks. Truck drivers stood talking with seeming indifference to the traffic trying to squeeze by. Local buses passed in the opposite direction, their conductors hanging out of the side doors giving hand signals to indicate their intentions.

The air was redolent with rich humus, rotting garbage, and diesel fumes. Old buildings sat side by side with new structures still under construction. Bamboo scaffold rose three or four storeys as renderers slathered on cement. In-between, deep green vegetation sought to retain its own space, growing tall toward the hot sun. Street vendors displayed wares laid out on cheap blue tarpaulins. Fruits and vegetables sitting side-by-side with 'knock-off' bags and 'designer' wear. Ice-cream sellers valiantly tried to pedal their carts along the rough and broken roads; the contents already beginning to melt.

At Dorje's instruction, the driver cut down an unmade back road. We bounced over a combination of potholes, piles of gravel and around sleeping homeless dogs dozing in the available shade. We passed a major concrete bridge with a distinct bow in the middle; presumably the result of a prior earthquake. Kathmandu is prone to some seismic activity which is most obvious in the older buildings. When I returned in 2011, we felt the tremors from the major earthquake in the far east of Nepal.

Having driven down assorted back roads and now thoroughly turned around, with the minivan taking a series of twisting turns, we eventually popped out in the western suburb of Chhauni near the foot of Swayambhunath (the Monkey Temple). It would become a landmark that would serve us well on this and subsequent visits. Within minutes we arrived at a brightly painted gateway. The street was relatively quiet compared to the other roads we had travelled, although taxis still plied their trade; tooting their horns as a friendly warning of their intent. Some military personnel wandered by, at this point I remembered from my previous research that Birendra Military Hospital and Chhauni Military Base were on this road.

From time to time, I would spot a small, khaki-coloured Suzuki van with a single light on the roof and a hand-painted red cross on the front. This appeared to be a military ambulance although there was nothing in the back of it. Patients would be forced to lie on a blanket while being transported. Equipment was not in evidence from what I could see through the windows as it would whip past us on the streets.

Our driver tooted his horn at the gateway of the Benchen Phuntsok Dargyeling (BPD) Monastery. The gates, swung open and we rolled into the forecourt. We were assailed by the bright golden yellow walls and blue trims of the various buildings. Potted marigolds lined the ramp to the next open space. While concreted, the area was swept clean and rubbish bins were in evidence. The sounds of the city receded as the chants of monks began to wash over us. A couple of homeless dogs lounged in the shade. A small cafe in the wall of the monastery sat off to our right. Beside it the Benchen Free Clinic operated for anyone in the area to access. Outside the wall motorbikes could be heard toot-tooting on the road as they passed each other.

We shouldered our bags and Dorje led the way up the ramp. Laughing children could be heard in the Benchen School. Passing between the various buildings in the delightful shade, we climbed a steep series of concrete stairs. Above us, outlined against the azure blue sky, rose the Benchen Vihar guesthouse. Climbing past dozens of giggling young boys attending the school in their burgundy robes, we exchanged 'hellos' and 'Namastes.' A couple of carpenters worked under a lean-to on the other side of the stairs. Pieces of furniture in various stages of construction leant against the concrete retaining wall. They would be used on the site of the monastery.

We passed through metal gates topped with wicked looking spikes and entered the gardens in front of the guesthouse. The spikes were an attempt to keep the ever present monkeys out of the grounds. An effort that invariably failed as the troupe passed through almost like clock-work every day, gingerly stepping over or around the obstructions.

I failed the first test of my training on day one. Reaching the top of the stairs, I was puffing like a steam train. I think we all were. Not surprisingly we were really sweating. Having left a cold early spring in Australia, we had arrived at the tail end of the monsoon season. Hot and steamy was the best way to describe it.

The entry level of the guesthouse switched from concrete slabs to sheets and tiles of creamy marble shot through with pale yellow lines set out in a welcoming pattern. Hip-high concrete hand rails held up by columns bordered the gardens of close-cut lawns and borders of flowering shrubs. Three plastic table and chair sets with brightly coloured umbrellas sat on the lawns. One was occupied by several visitors as they sipped on cups of tea. A woman in traditional dress was sweeping the marble with a hand-made broom. The walls were painted yellow while the window sills and trims were a dark red. A rich brown polished wooden door step led into the reception area.

While Dorje spoke with the reception desk staff, we were able to take in the broad expanse of the capital laid out before us. We could see through the hazy air all the way across to the eastern mountains surrounding the Kathmandu Valley. In the distance, planes could be seen heading in and out of the airport. A spire or minaret rose above the centre of the city. Expected clouds hung heavily along the distant mountain ranges.

A vegetarian kitchen and dining room was off to the left of reception, an internet room and laundry off to the right.

Signing in, we were given our room keys each on a large, engraved brass tag. Our room, 105, was on the first floor directly over the reception desk. Paying only a few dollars a day, we weren't expecting the Hilton and yet we were pleasantly surprised.

Inside the room with its pale yellow walls, there were two single beds with their own night stands and a communal telephone. A full self-contained tiled bathroom took up about a third of the room. Its only draw-back was several holes in the wall granting access to the rusty stop-cock. Fresh white towels hung neatly folded on the towel rail, a small bar of soap still wrapped in its box sat on the glass shelf under the mirror.

The main room held one small timber desk. On it sat a form to order laundry service. A backless chair peeked from underneath. Looking fairly plain, a short-pile, serviceable carpet covered the floor. Light-weight curtains could be drawn across the windows although they would not be able to cut off the bright, northern light. Another timber and glass door led onto a common balcony across the front of the building; again covered in marble.

Warning signs were posted against leaving doors open and unguarded. The monkeys are notorious room thieves with a history of trashing rooms like a proverbial rock star. Anything purple seems to take their fancy as it resembles the purple flowers growing locally which have a narcotic effect on them. They also warned against feeding them as it leads to aggressive behaviour against the guests.

All in all, the accommodation was actually quite comfy; cool enough in the hot weather with a ceiling fan to circulate the air, rooms were cleaned daily and all the rhesus macaque monkeys you can laugh at. Power points were available but were often placed in inconvenient places such as in the hallway but not near the beds.

After some freshening up in the rooms, we met downstairs in the gardens where we shared masala tea and snacked on a new treat called momos. A momo is a type of steamed dumpling which can have a variety of fillings. They are often served with a dipping sauce, perhaps a spicy ketchup or similar. I have on occasion also eaten them deep fried after steaming. A dozen make an excellent light meal when you might not be able to face anything else. Kim particularly enjoyed the chewy covering with the flavoursome, spiced vegetable filling.

Image: Kim Stanley-Eyles

We discussed our plans for the following days. Our shopping needs, money exchange, provisioning, and even the trekking permits and porters insurance all needed attending to. These days trekking companies are required to insure their porters in case the worst happens. This way the families are given some compensation should something occur. To my interest, it seemed that the coverage included the time from payments up to the start of the trek as well. Should a porter be injured once they were booked but before the journey started, their family would still be compensated. The ethical individual traveller will consider this a vital requirement. In fact, I am fairly certain that you cannot get your trekking permits without proof of insurance. Dorje handled all of these details for us.

Having eaten some local food and enjoyed our tea (they love their tea in Nepal), Dorje took us up to Swayambhunath, or The Monkey Temple. This magnificent temple complex covers the whole of the hill top. It covers four or five acres although I am not sure how accurate that is. Large families of monkeys live on or journey to the hill and receive some fairly generous food offerings from the worshiping locals. Rising above the valley floor, you can see nearly 360 degree views over Kathmandu.

We climbed one of the many steep stairways with many stops to watch the antics of the monkeys. One group of kids was making great use of the hand rails, using crushed soft drink bottles as a sled to slide as far down the hill as they could, giggling the whole time. We paused in the shade of some tall trees while

Sandra attempted to get some photos. Local feral dogs lazily looked us over as potential benefactors of food but gave it up as too much effort in the midday heat.

Ever present around the complex were long strings of coloured prayer flags. These flags flap and flutter in the breeze taking their prayers to the heavens. Like some brightly coloured spider web, they stretch in every direction. Trees seemingly vanish under the mass of material. Some have been up for so long that the colours have faded to see-through scraps; the prayers printed on them relegated to mere shadows.

A bald monk in short burgundy robes sat beside a stall selling slices of intensely white coconut; a gentle smile on his face. His simple sandals were a contrast to the modern watch on his wrist. A short bamboo pole above the metal table held a small multi-coloured umbrella.

Dozens if not hundreds of people had joined us on the hill top to watch the sun go down. Here a family took photos, there two young lovers stood chastely near each other admiring the view. Devotees said prayers and rang bells. Lines of prayer wheels were spun by hand as each person passed to the left in a clock-wise motion; lips moving with soft murmuring of prayers, repeated for each wheel turned.

A man sat on the stone steps leaning against a carved stone lion with a rice bag, handing out small offerings to a grey, male rhesus monkey that chittered at him for taking too long to feed him. It screeched and made feints in an effort to make the man work faster. The man smiled gently at it, tentatively moving to gently stroke the monkey's fur. This seemed a brave or foolish act since the monkey could move at blinding speed and inflict severe damage with teeth and fingers. It often slapped at him and made aggressive sounds.

Wandering the temple complex, I was surprised that amongst these ancient brick buildings were tucked small shops catering to the pilgrims and tourists. Cheap, badly made trinkets sat side by side with elaborate art works. CD stands vied with quilted rug makers; their simple, gentle prayer songs were a contrast with the visual beauty of elaborate quilts. Stalls sold brass cups to hold butter candles used for devotions in the many temples. Street hawkers were on the lookout for tourists like us but we managed to avoid most of them. We didn't have any local currency to spend at that stage until after we had been to the money changers in Thamel.

Children ran backwards and forwards in games of 'chasey,' or flew kites while watched over by the Buddha eyes of the white and gold Stupa. Evidence of fresh white-washing was present on some of the structures. I found it stunning that some of the temple buildings can be dated back over 1,500 years.

Kim caught the eye of some young women looking out over the throng from their second storey ancient carved window. They waved and smiled, and the tiny kittens they were cuddling suddenly were bobbed up and down along the window sill in a pretend dance. As Kim laughed, the women gently made the kittens wave back, also laughing.

Image: Kim
Stanley-Eyles

We descended the steep "Stairs to Swayambhunath" which initially felt almost vertical. I felt sorry for the pilgrims climbing the stairs. Half way down sat a small hooded, grubby, dark-skinned beggar. I had not seen her sitting there until a chilling single word passed her lips as I went past. She said "hello" with all the sorrow of the world contained in it. It was the only word in English she seemed to know. I learnt a hard lesson that day. Despite how hard it is walk by, you cannot help every single person. To stop is to invite waves of other beggars to begin following you, blocking your path and pulling at your clothes. Better to find a project which can provide ongoing support to a wide range of people. This is precisely what we would be considering by the end of our journey.

Heavy clouds began to form on the boundary of the valley. Distant rumbles a mere back note to the vehicle traffic. As the afternoon wore on, the atmospheric conditions suggested that we were in for a good thunderstorm. The rumbles became grumbles which became cracks and booms. With the clouds closing in, the city became dark and the lightning show was spectacular. Forks both thick and thin struck down across the city in the nightly show. Since I am a great fan of such powerful shows of nature, it was a truly amazing sight to behold.

Following the roads back to the monastery, we ate a light meal and retired for the evening. The nightly tropical downpour washed the city clean for us. Thunder rumbled across the city as we fell into a deep slumber.

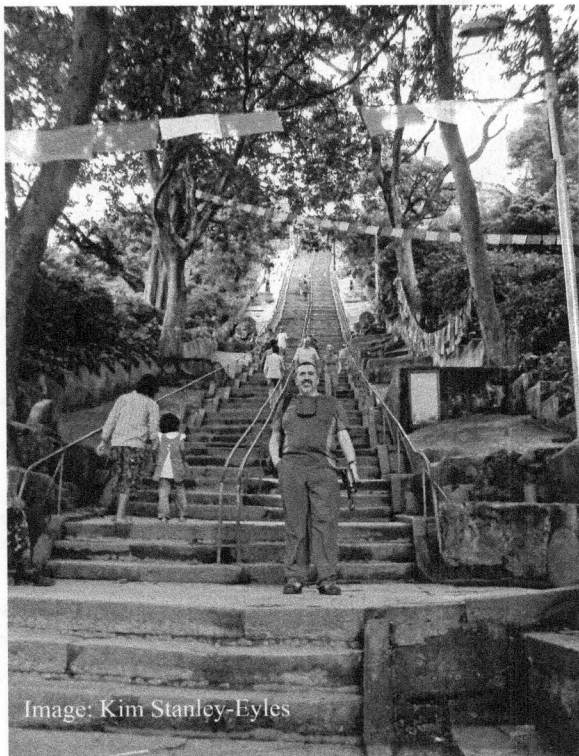

Image: Kim Stanley-Eyles

While Kim slept on, I was wide awake the next morning at about 05:30 local time. For such a large city, Kathmandu was very quiet. The occasional screech alerted me to some territorial argument between the monkeys. A few minutes later, the sergeant down on the military base began bellowing at the troops. A bugle played reveille in the manner of buglers the world over. After a short cacophony, the sounds of the city drifted back into a gentle hubbub as people began to wake.

I slipped out of the room and made my way to the highest floor of the guesthouse so that I could get some images and video over the roof tops. Passing very close by one of the male monkeys, I had to appear as non-threatening as possible since he was looking for a fight. From my vantage point over the city, I could see the fascination my monkey companions had with the view. Two of them sat on the handrail and gazed down on the buildings below. So beautiful! A deep gong rang below me and was joined by the sonorous voices of the monks in early Morning Prayer. The shouts of soldiers doing their morning exercises worked in counter point to the relaxing chants from the temple below.

We enjoyed a breakfast of scrambled eggs, some sweetish toast, the Nepali version of hash browns and a pot of 'Nescaf.' Mangal, a friend of Mike and Margaret's, came to visit. He spoke about our upcoming journey. Mangal was already booked for another trek so would not be journeying with us this time.

With the promise of some cheap and engaging shopping, we departed after breakfast for the tourist district of Thamel. The previous night's rain made the walking slippery and we constantly dodged being splashed by passing vehicles. Pausing at the end of the first road, Margaret stopped at a shop to get a new battery fitted in her watch. Taking a few moments, I filmed the street in an arc from the up-hill streets past the taxi rank down towards a nearby market place.

Despite the pervasive odour of rotting vegetation and rubbish in the streets, from time to time we would pass spice stores and mills. The scents of bay leaves, chilli, cinnamon, cloves, cumin, ginger, nigella, peppercorns, saffron, and turmeric were almost stereotypical of Asia and yet distinctly Nepalese. It was the smell of freshly made curry pastes and the seasoning of flavoursome dishes. These spices appeared in just about every dish; sometimes at the start after being dry roasted or fried to release the aromatics, or added ground in the finishing stages. From my own personal experience, while chilli was often added to a lot of dishes, it was quite possible to obtain almost the same flavour without it. Since returning, I have made use of my favourite cookbook and conversations with its author to try and recreate some of my favourite meals.

Proceeding through back streets with which we would soon become very familiar, occasionally we would pass small Hindu shrines outside shops and homes. What ground was safe to walk on, was often shared with the cars and bikes travelling in both directions. Tall walls surrounded some of the homes making the road even narrower. Taking a branch to the left, we parted from the road and walked down a narrow lane. At the far end, a short but steep set of stairs brought us back to the road. The stone stairs had been worn down by thousands of feet requiring careful use of the handrails to negotiate them. We rejoined the road opposite a local butcher. Whole carcasses hang out the front in the sun. The flesh was reddening in the heat while the butchers chopped them up for orders from the trickle of customers passing by.

Sloppy mud over-flowed from the various potholes as we navigated Swayambhu Marg East towards the city and across the rubbish-strewn banks of the Vishnumati River. Someone's sow wallowed in the mud. Several piglets squealed amongst the low plants beside the water. Various cows wandered or sat on the bridge. We negotiated an unmade five-way intersection by dodging cars and sliding through the thin soup of mud. In the centre of this chaos, a road crew dug a large pit in the middle of the intersection between Swayambhu Marg and Puspalal Path. The amount of mud being removed was only just staying ahead of the liquid slop pouring back in.

Selecting a side road, Mike confidently led us along another road, taking us further away from heavy traffic. I remembered the motorbikes and scooters weaving their way amongst the pedestrians. Around us, amongst the heavy foot traffic, we saw children dressed immaculately for school and stepping deftly around the mud. Somehow they managed to stay clean. From the youngest to the eldest, they proudly wore the school uniforms and marched with purpose to their various classrooms. We passed some schools that appeared to be built right beside the footpath/street with no playing grounds. The children would wave to us through the barred, apparently glassless windows as we walked past. Overhead, the chatter of excited young children announced a pre-school above one of the shops. Even though it was Sunday, the kids were still attending school.

At street level, tradesmen worked on a new multi-storey building whilst labourers moved piles of recycled bricks. In a nearby brick-paved water access point below the level of the street, locals were doing their washing and hanging it from lines strung between the trees.

After a wrong turn at the five-way intersection between Gangalal Marga and JP Road, we eventually made our way onto JP Road in Thamel. From there, in due course, we found our next stop. Weizen Bakery sat in a recessed courtyard garden opposite a shop selling musical instruments. The front contained a bakery shop which attracted a roaring trade also well known for its evening clearance sales. Behind, chairs and tables abounded either in the open or under sturdy covers. At the very back, next to the kitchen was an enclosed dining room.

Image: Sandra Gormley

Mike and I found a travel booking office where we exchanged a few dollars into rupee so that we could eat and buy some drinks. The hopeful office worker looked a little disappointed when we explained we were already booked onto a trek. As we left the office, his eyes lit up hoping we might come to see him when we returned from the trek to organise a flight over the Kathmandu Valley.

It was at Weizen Bakery that Dorje caught up with us, a shy and cheeky young man behind him. All angles, lean and wiry this was Kanchha one of our porters and Dorje's brother-in-law. He had a glint of mischief in his eye and Kim knew that she would get along famously with him.

First things first, we had to change more of our money. Kim and I wanted to convert some of our Australian dollars. To cover our expenses and emergencies, we changed $AU2,200 and walked out with a monstrous pile of cash which worked out to be 146,000 Nepali rupees (NPR).

The next stop was a trekking outfitter on Thamel Marg who, it turned out, was a neighbour of Dorje here in the capital. Dorje had left us to obtain the permits and insurance so we had no interpreter.

In the cramped, warm store, we carefully inspected and bought two huge backpacks, a day pack for me, a pair of trekking pants for Kim, a drinking bottle and two good quality ponchos. It was the first time we had ever haggled and I'm not certain to this day if we had caused any insult with our initial price. But we were 'playing the game' of haggling and they seemed to accept that we were trying. Given the lack of each other's language, the process involved the sharing of a calculator. As each of us came up with a price, it would be typed in and the calculator passed across. With waving of hands, a new number would be entered before being passed back. Eventually we settled on a price of 23,000 rupees for all of the items. That was the equivalent of one brand new, decent back pack in Australia at $AU350; the price of one decent backpack in Australia. We also hired two brand new down sleeping bags for the duration of the trek.

During the process of trying out items, a young girl about maybe three years of age entered the shop. She had an angelic face if somewhat grubby. She smiled and walked up to each of us wordlessly holding out her hand. Sadly the fingers were all missing or stubs; the survivor of leprosy or some other such tragedy. Here was a three year old begging for money. The owner of the shop intercepted her and ushered her outside gently. I didn't see it but I was told that he gave her some money and sent her on her way. Such a shame that there is no support network for her although cynics might suggest that begging would earn much more money from rich foreigners.

There appears to be a bit of an understanding when you haggle. If you give a bit of ground on your final price, then everyone saves face. We were invited to then sit down and share tea with the shop owners. This was a sign that we had acted honourably. A staff member was directed to head out and purchase drinks for everyone. Seating was on low woven stools. To everyone's amusement, including my own, I immediately fell off the back and onto the floor.

Heading out into the street, we walked to some nearby shops to purchase maps, badges, sundry other items including a prayer bell for Kim. She intended to use it at the Thorung La pass, the highest point we would reach on this trip at 5,416 metres. In memory of her late mother, Kim was going to ring the bell into the wind before taking the bell home and placing it next to the one her mother had owned.

No visit to Kathmandu is complete without a visit to each of the three Durbar Squares, one for each of the three ancient kingdoms. On this day, we were able to visit Hanuman Dhoka Durbar Square which is within easy walking distance south of Thamel.

Through a warm rain, the group wandered the bustling, stone-paved streets. A young boy in a chequered, pale yellow shirt latched onto Mike trying to sell him something or another. His English was good as was his geography, picking up that we were Australian. Whatever he was selling, the price kept getting cheaper and cheaper until Kim and I thought he was not making any profit at all. Undeterred and with a cheeky grin, he dodged off to begin spruiking his wares to another tourist.

Weaving through traffic and turning corners, we came into Hanuman Dhoka Durbar Square via Gangalal Marga (road) as the showers cleared. Overcast but warm, the sight was amazing. Dotted throughout the square paved in large flag stones, were multi-storey structures. They were made from handmade bricks and decorated with stone and timber carvings. Purchasing our tickets for the sum of 300 rupees, we wandered left into the main part of the square. Some of the structures showed signs of repair; often as the result of previous earthquakes in the region. The ridge line of an old tiled roof meandered drunkenly; evidence of one of the prior earthquakes. A small temple poked out from the buttressed roots of a tree which had grown up and through its roof. Like the other squares in the valley, this one is a World Heritage site and as we wandered from building to building, we could see why. Some were relatively recent from the 1700's while others were 400-500 years old. Research suggests that this site may have been in use as far back as the third century.

The square contains the Kumari Ghar, the home of the Kumari or living goddess. We had missed the celebrations by a few days when she was carried forth from her home and around the square on a giant covered wagon. She is seen at the window sometimes during the day for lucky devotees but she is normally isolated from the rest of the world. Non-Hindus are not supposed to take a photo of her in the Kumari Ghar. Vendors sold postcards of her outside the entrance of her palace.

Given the high visitor numbers, the street hawkers were in abundance and descended on us like flies. Kim became deeply engrossed in a conversation with a man selling wooden flutes. Often poor flute sellers would wander the streets trying to sell their wares. As an incentive, they will play selected tunes on them.

There is an unexpected beauty in the notes they produce. I was often curious as to why orchestras around the world had not snapped these people up. Despite being poor, they could make a fortune just busking in the streets instead.

We tried to be as polite as possible in refusing the offer to buy the other cheaply made trinkets. Previous advice had suggested that it was better to ignore them rather than engage in conversation but it's hard to break years of training to be polite. Once they realised we were Australian, it was amazing how many of them had friends and relatives in Brisbane, or Melbourne, or Sydney.

In between showers, we all tried to get the perfect shots on our various cameras.

Leaving north by Hanuman Dhoka Road, we returned to Thamel as the showers began again. Through the series of dark, narrow, rain soaked streets we worked our way back to the bustling five-way intersection of Gangalal Marga and JP Road. As the rain became heavier, Dorje arranged for several taxis to take us back to BPD Monastery. While waiting, two primary school aged girls in the back of a broken down van tried to practise their English on us with much giggling on both sides. The other ten kids shyly listened but didn't join us in the chat.

Bundled into the battered vehicles, windows steaming up on a regular basis, we took a fascinating 11 minute journey. "Welcome to Kathmandu," chuckled Mike to our video camera as we bounced over potholes and navigated the muddy, slick roads.

It seemed like the car was 4-wheel driving at times. Negotiating the intersection at Swayambhu Marg and Puspalal Path, I noted that the workers had abandoned the large hole which was rapidly filling with muddy water. Vehicles were coming from all directions but we managed to get through the morass. Climbing up on to the bridge, our taxi then navigated around other vehicles on the narrow roads before depositing us back at the gates of the monastery. We unloaded our booty and retreated to our rooms. Tomorrow we would begin the trek.

Chapter 4 - The rise of the Thorung Five

"One's destination is never a place, but a new way of seeing things." – Henry Miller

Before the sun was up, a text message came through from Australia. It was ten minutes to four in the morning in Kathmandu or about five minutes past eight in Australia. I was wide awake. Morning prayers started not long after. The low, sonorous voices drifted gently up from the monastery to the guesthouse. The date was September 7th.

Slowly the day began. The morning bugler blurted out the call for soldiers to present themselves for physical training. Rising, I found that our washing had failed to dry properly. The night had been full of the monsoon rain leaving everything humid.

We met the team of boys down in the forecourt after breakfast. Our minivan arrived just before 08:00. In a light smattering of rain, the van was loaded and we all packed tightly into the seats. There we were: Mike, Margaret, Sandra, Kim and I with Dorje, Dhan, Kanchha, La Har and Purna.

The boys, as they became known, settled in for the long drive. Kanchha and Dhan settled in for a snooze. I juggled the day pack and my video camera. Recording a short commentary with Kim, I then used it to catch the scenes of traffic. The morning traffic jam had already started and it took some time for us to weave through the outer suburbs. Once again trucks, buses and the assortment of two- and four-wheeled transports jostled for a position in the lanes actually moving forward. More than once we would find the front grill of a truck peering in our side windows.

Crossing Ring Road we headed west on Kalankisthan Road past the Armed Police Force Barracks and Hospital and the Nepal Telecom Satellite Earth Station rising up the sides of the valley. From our vantage point, we could look back over the brick factories and open farm lands that have not yet been absorbed into the sprawling city. Further from the centre of the city, I noted that the buildings often fronted directly onto the road. Very few of them were residential, being more industrial in nature. Leaving the suburb of Thankot, the buildings were more widely spaced as the road rose to the rim of the valley. The humid, hazy air was making it difficult to see more than a few kilometres back towards the city. We passed quickly through the Nagdhunga Check Point and began the winding descent into the next valley on the Tribhuvan Rajpath.

Almost immediately we hit a traffic jam. Clouds hung low around and below us. From our vantage point, we could see through the drifting clouds the switchback roads directly below us choked with vehicles of all sizes. Drifting up the slope with the clouds were the warbling notes of the various truck horns. This traffic jam was obviously a known and regular occurrence as evidenced by the number of passengers who disembarked vehicles, lit cigarettes or began urinating over the sides of the road. Beside the road on up-slope side was a one-metre deep gutter. At its base, gravel and small rocks were washed over by a steady stream of water coming off the hill side. Occasional light showers added to the flow. The air was surprisingly warm with a mix of jungle rot and diesel fumes.

Mike invited me to sit up front between him and the driver so I could film things better. Eventually we began moving down-hill, squeezing past heavily laden trucks wheezing up the hill into Kathmandu; the loads often including one or more labourers sitting on top. The cabs of the trucks were brightly coloured and draped with bunting or prayer flags, or covered in chrome like metal sheeting like giant mirror pieces. Mixtures of words either in English or Devangari proclaimed nice messages like 'Live Love Life' or 'Love Father' and adorned the spare flat spaces around the trucks. The ubiquitous 'Horn Please' was plastered across the back of trucks and buses everywhere.

Eventually we snaked down the steep hill, passing a series of broken down vehicles often with the local police admonishing the drivers for their careless failure to maintain their transport. On some corners, evidence of recent landslides coated the road while any large rocks had been push to the sides.

Breaking free of the mess, the van travelled along the highway. We passed an ambulance actually under lights and siren as it tried to squeeze its way back up the hill to Kathmandu. During the early part of the journey, we noted five different vehicles that had crashed into the embankment; the axles often resting on the road with wheels trapped in the one metre deep gutters. Some were in a worse state than others. One truck appeared to have rolled over with the cab crushed almost beyond recognition. The ambulance had possibly come from one of these collisions.

Turning onto the Prithvi Rajmarga (or highway) we continued west. After a couple of hours on the road, we stopped for brunch at Hamlet Restaurant. Its car park was already packed with five large modern coaches and some motorbikes. A steady stream of vehicles cruised past in either direction. Above us the clouds hovered below the crests of the mountains.

The food was good local fare if somewhat spicy. After a quick toilet stop, we climbed back aboard the mini-bus. Moving on, we passed settlements ranging from squalid shanty towns to neat and orderly homes. Around all of them, poultry could normally be seen scratching on the road side. Occasionally goats could be seen tethered near the homes. At one point, another ambulance was spotted sitting in a ford over the highway while the driver washed it. Apart from isolated stretches of potholes, often the road was in a reasonable state. In need of repair, certainly, but still the driver was able to obtain a passable speed. The further from Kathmandu, the larger the damaged areas were even though attempts had been made to repair them. We were often being overtaken on blind corners by motorbikes with pillion passengers. Passing through towns where the road was often narrow, oncoming traffic would force us to come to a complete stop behind local buses. While we were never accosted, the buses would be inundated by street vendors with bags of fairy floss (a local favourite?) and fruits. The passengers would be buying the wares directly through their windows on either side of the bus. Local dogs would dive out from between these vehicles forcing our driver to slam on his squeaking brakes.

At Dumre, we turned right and, crossing the swollen Seti River, began driving north up the Dumre – Besi Sahar – Chame Highway. Frequently we would overtake local buses stopped in towns only to encounter a vehicle coming from the other direction. With much tooting of horns, the drivers seemed to have a way of negotiating who had right of way. There was regularly a man who would hang out the door of a bus and wave on another vehicle to pass if his vehicle was slower.

The road varied in condition from sealed to potholed and all the scales in between. Various buses and mini vans were our companions on the road. Some were loaded up on the roof with luggage. Others were carrying passengers up top. In one case we saw a Spanish couple perched on the roof of a mini-bus. They would become occasional companions on the trek. Verdant mountains rose on both sides of us. The greenery began to close in on all sides. The air smelt sweet and fresh with the hint of natural decay only achieved in healthy ecosystems. Cool through the open windows, the breeze held the promise of rain even if it didn't deliver.

Image: Sandra Gormley

We eventually began to snake alongside the mighty Marsyangdi Nadi (river) at the peak of monsoon flood. The ever present rumble of water was a sub note anytime we were not moving.

Sometime around 14:00 we arrived in the town of Besi Sahar (830 metres) where we were to leave our motorised transport. A light spitting of rain was falling as our bags were unloaded from the minivan. Overhead a rooster crowed from the low hanging power lines. The streets were a bustle of activity as the locals went about their business barely paying us any attention, so used are they to foreigners.

Besi Sahar is the starting point of the Annapurna Circuit trek. The general advice is for trekkers to travel anti-clockwise as it is considered the easiest way to undertake the walk. During peak season, this town would normally be packed with trekkers eager to begin their journey.

Dorje, as guide, was responsible for our travel documents and made his way to the police check post to register our arrival, while we retreated to the Mongolian Guesthouse for some tea and bananas.

Each of us had been issued with a Registration Card from the government run Trekkers Information Management System (TIMS) and an Entry Permit to the Annapurna Conservation Area issued by the National Trust for Nature Conservation. We would be required to present these at each Tourist Check Point along the journey. These permits allow for tracking of visitors in case of emergencies. Part of the fees for the permits goes towards insurance for the porters and guides. This was something in times past that had not been available. Porters injured or killed while working had no recompense for their families.

Less than an hour later we were ready to depart. Ever ready to experiment, I was wearing a heart rate monitor linked to my wrist watch to track how I was travelling. This would warn me if my rate rose too quickly or remain too high for an extended period.

Each of the porters was individually allocated to members of our group. I was lucky that Dorje had elected to also act as my porter. Kim teamed up with La Har, Mike with Kanchha, Margaret with Purna and Sandra with Dhan. After briefly stopping for a group photo, we headed down over a small river and crossed our first bamboo bridge. In high spirits, we walked along the gravel road into the wild back country of Nepal.

The first day's walk was a mild three hours of gentle rolling land following the banks of the Marsyangdi Nadi. We passed through Shahaji, crossing over another bamboo bridge after having stopped in the cooling shade of a Bodhi tree for refreshments. It was here that Mike shared some biscuits with an elderly couple. Tempting vistas of the snow covered mountain ranges could be glimpsed between the nearby jungle shrouded peaks. Low fluffy clouds hung between. The air was warm and humid but not stifling.

Image: Margaret Evans

I was feeling good. My training seemed to have paid off as I opened my legs into a comfortable stride. My daypack adjusted properly on my shoulders, hiking pole swinging in my hand and large waist-band first aid kit, the walking came easily. Revelling in the grand scenery around me, I was ready to take on the world. Each breath of fresh air charging my batteries, I felt like I could walk for ever.

The group had already strung out along the trail. Passing through the villages of Chanaute, Sera, Mahathok, and Dhan we crossed a series of bridges ranging from bamboo to steel suspension. At first the hanging bridges were a considerable personal challenge, especially the first one with its worn wooden treads that was alarmingly missing every few planks giving us with an incredible view of the flooded river far below our feet.

Image: Kim Stanley-Eyles

After this one, the old style rope and plank style, subsequent bridges seemed to have been completely replaced by modern steel cable and mesh which seemed a great deal more reassuring, although they still swung and bounced wildly with every step. Along the way we marvelled at the hand construction of a new road bridge. Reaching Khudi and with cool of the late afternoon beginning to increase, we crossed our last suspension bridge of the day into Bhulbhule (840 metres) at around 18:00.

Our accommodation overlooked the river which rumbled comfortingly in its flood. It was a two storey building for the actual guest rooms and a separate structure which was the 'dinning' room. We began to notice a charming literalisation of English words which, while not correct, was almost always apparent by its meaning.

The room that we had been assigned was basic in a way that we would find consistent for the remainder of our stay; small but serviceable rooms with basic light and a power point. Flat timber beds with thin foam mattresses which would come to feel surprisingly pleasant after a day's hard trekking. The bathroom facilities were common to the floor we were on but did have a seated toilet. Locks, barely capable of securing a room, were supplied although once inside, you had to rely on a small slide bolt that would be hard pressed to keep anyone out.

Having a meal in the 'dinning' room downstairs, we all retreated to our rooms for an early night in anticipation of hard walking the next day. Here we had daal bhaat for the first time. To the rumble of the river Kim and I began to nod off even though I was trying hard to update my diary and type up a blog entry. Mosquitos outside the windows did not appear to gain entrance during the night. Just in case, Kim had a mosquito head net to sleep in as they find her particularly tasty.

Day two of the trek should have been a nice early start with breakfast and then onto the trail. Today was the day that we would discover Nepal is the land of the broken thong (flip flop, jandal, etc.) as we were constantly finding single ones either intact or broken and discarded along the paths. It almost became a game to count how many we found between rest stops although that quickly began to pale as there were so many.

Having ordered breakfast, we sat waiting in the dining room. We shared our stories with other guests while we waited. After an hour, nothing had arrived. Dorje came to our rescue and organised our food. Again there was literalisation this time in the food being served. My banana pancake turned out to be just that; a cake about 5 centimetres thick cooked in a fry pan. It was delicious but just too thick for my liking and was unable to finish it off.

Dorje was able to explain why our food had been delayed. Both the mother and daughter who ran the establishment had come down with typhoid overnight. After offering some of our medical supplies, he explained that they already had medicine.

The morning was warm and steamy even though the cloud cover was still in place. Having packed our bags we took time to watch a young mother teach her toddler to walk... on the suspension bridge. While hanging on to the mother's hands, the youngster was already beginning to find the steady feet for which the Nepali are renowned. As we waited for the others in our group to be ready, two young boys crossed the bridge. Halfway across, they encountered a loaded donkey train heading in the opposite direction. Rather than back up so the donkeys could pass, the boys deftly squatted down as each animal approached allowing the pack animals unimpeded movement. In this way travel in both directions was achieved.

The donkeys carried two bags of grain each. Their owner wandered along at the tail end of the train encouraging the old, lazy or inexperienced animals with a bamboo switch. Those in the lead knew their destination well and followed the path unerringly.

With everyone in tow, we departed after the donkeys. Climbing a series of well fitted stone stairs, we passed along a narrow path between the close buildings built into the steep slopes. Dorje peeled off at a local shop to purchase some 'plastics' for the rest of the boys. My initial confusion cleared as I understood he was buying large blue rubbish bags into which would be cut a neck and arm holes. These would be worn over the top of our backpacks to keep them dry should it begin to rain. Luckily we had all bought backpacks that had in-built rain covers anyway, and our ponchos purchased from Thamel were large enough to go over us and our daypacks if needed.

Leaving the village behind, we travelled along a well maintained path beside the east bank of the river. Our only obstructions were a series of low-pressure water pipes that came in from up slope and delivered constantly running water to the various houses and farms along the way. After more than seven years of drought at home, it almost felt obscene to see taps constantly left running and water flowing away down slope. Above us to the right, a high waterfall dropped hundreds of metres to our level of the valley. It finally dawned on me that we were in a country where rainfall was a bigger issue than drought.

The first bridge of the day was constructed of three bamboo shafts lashed together. It flexed alarmingly as I put my weight on it but gathering my nerve, I crossed it quickly to a smattering of applause from our porters. They already had the measure of my nervousness.

Terraces of rice paddies rose steeply up the side of the valley. Boundary lines of beans grew in each embankment. The rice grew lush and waved in the gentle breeze. Hiding behind the ever present clouds, the sun provided a gentle but persistent warmth.

During one of our rest stops, we encountered a young woman tucked in amongst some rocks. She was harvesting mud into a woven basket. This seemed an unusual thing to do but on careful questioning, she explained that it was for the floor of her hut. It would compact well to make a smooth, hard floor.

Following the trail we passed a side branch that climbed the hillside. Discussion broke out as to whether we followed our existing wide path or climb up. The group split up as La Har was insistent that up was the correct path. We carried on as before but only lasted a few minutes when the road ceased to exist. A landslide from the night before had removed all traces. Back tracking slightly, the decision was made that we would climb straight up through the jungle. Margaret managed to capture a shot as we ploughed our way amongst the vines and thickly growing jungle. We did some serious 'bush bashing' and at times vines were being used as handrails. Pushing our way through, we eventually met the others when we came out on a stretch of newly constructed road. After a quick leech check, we were on our way again.

My exhaustion after such a simple climb was a warning sign of the potential health issues to come. From that point we took lots of rest stops. The workload increased as we began to encounter more landslides. As the clouds began to clear, the heat and humidity began to rise. The heat rapidly became oppressive combined with high humidity, lack of shade and minimal breeze. I was quickly heading towards heat exhaustion. While in its grip, I did not recognise that I was becoming dehydrated. I was carrying three litres of water and I had drunk the lot by lunch time. It was all being sweated out. Despite Mike's suggestion, I had been unable to locate powdered rehydration products in the supermarket before we left.

With several more climbs to go, I was travelling slower and slower. As everyone had reached our lunchtime stop, the boys came back down the trail, relieved me of my day pack and encouraged me to walk slowly with lots of rest stops along the way. Eventually I joined everyone else in the village of Bahundanda (1310 metres). Mike insisted that I strip back as many items of clothing as reasonable. My boots being removed were the biggest relief. I took on a fair amount of fluid. The decision was made to hold over in the ridge top village and take lunch there. We discussed where we would aim for today since our original destination of Syange would not be feasible by night fall.

The afternoon storm came early and made the decision easy for us. It would be too dangerous to walk on. From the dining room of the Hotel Superb View we watched the storm come racing down the valley. Within 30 minutes, it had covered the six or so kilometres from Syange, blanketing everything in an impenetrable grey wall of rain. Around us thunder rumbled in the warm air. Mike snoozed on the floor of the room. Sandra made notes of the journey. Kim and I began speaking with Paru, the wife of the hotel owner. She was intrigued by the soft toy bears we had with us; each in the livery of Rural Ambulance Victoria and the Country Fire Authority. Hovering in the background was Kishor, a 17 year old school boy, who worked at the hotel.

When asking if we could donate supplies to the "medical hall" we had seen as we had entered the town, Paru explained that Doctor Sunil Tiwari ran a medical centre. We asked to meet him and he dutifully appeared after the rain stopped. While we didn't have much to offer, we gave him two bundles of supplies which he carefully went through. Some items he asked for explanations while for others he understood and described their use to Paru. She was most intrigued with the plastic umbilical clamps and became quite animated when their purpose was explained. Dr. Tiwari accepted the bundles but was more interested in seeing if we had any medications to offer. Often the supplies he orders are waylaid and never arrive, appearing instead on the black market. We were neither qualified to supply nor did we have any items available so he gave us a list of medications. Sadly the list went missing before we could consider finding a way to fill it. Dr. Tiwari services a population of 3,000 including outlying farms. On average he sees 20 patients a day. He told us that he had been the village doctor for about eight years.

When the rain had eased, and after much badgering by Kishor, Kim, Margaret, Sandra and I wandered down to see his school. It was a combined primary and high school servicing grades one to 12 with around 400 students. The rooms were very basic with earth floors, no heating or air conditioning, and no glass windows. Each room was fitted with a central light bulb and a blackboard. The school hours were 10:00-16:00 and some students had up to two hours walk each way. At one end of the central, bare earth quadrangle was an open stage where the children would learn and practise traditional music and dance.

A canteen was available for students to buy their lunch. There was no one around when we visited.

It was exam time and in some of the rooms, the desks were labelled with chalk markings at every seat. Instead of students from one year level sitting in the same room, they would be interspersed with students from other years. The markings represented year level and student number. Cheating would be well-nigh impossible in these circumstances.

Kishor did try asking us up for money to buy text books but we knew that 15,000 rupees was too much for three books. He eventually admitted that it was for five books "and a little for me." We only said we would consider helping if his headmaster emailed Margaret with the required books details. We would then chip in to buy them and have them sent to Kishor. Not surprisingly, we never heard from the headmaster.

We then went to a teahouse where Paru proudly showed us her new large gleaming silver refrigerator that had been manhandled to the village along the same trails we had used.

This was the second such fridge. The first was in the dining room of our hotel. Paru unexpectedly gifted Kim with a locally made cotton wrap skirt with a great deal of laughing and goodwill; Paru was just over 5 foot tall and very slender, Kim is 5' 8" with a farmer's daughters frame. Finding one to fit was fun for all.

The Hotel Superb View has a sign that proudly states "not rec by the Lonely Planet Guide Book" although we never did get an explanation about that claim. We did, however, have excellent mobile reception as the elements were right outside our window and aimed straight into our room.

September 9th dawned clear if somewhat moist. I hadn't slept much overnight; the heat exhaustion taking its toll on me. The previous day's rain had cleared the air. From our view on the ridge top, we could see towards our destination. Gathering our possessions, we headed off down the slippery steps and paving. Joining the trail, the boys took their appointed places beside or nearby each of us. Even shy Purna made sure that we would always have someone to call on should the need arise.

Margaret's camera was working overtime as she documented some of the glorious plants and flowers along the way. In between the exotic flowers and ferns were identifiable wild versions of geranium and garlic.

Mike stretched out his long legs and strode forward with Kanchha happily in tow. As we walked, I asked Dorje about local snakes. In the Terai, the jungle/forest zone along the entire southern border of Nepal, a python could be found capable of attacking humans. Where we were, there was one deadly snake; a pit viper which can apparently kill in 24 hours.

After about 45 minutes we found a good reason why we needed to have stopped the day before. A large portion of the track had disappeared in a landslide. Chances were high that it had happened late yesterday afternoon during the storm and would have taken us with it if we had kept going. Some brave locals and a few reckless trekkers were wading through the deep, soft, oozing mud that appeared to be still in motion. The trekkers had at least removed their boots which were hanging around their necks by the knotted laces. We elected to go up and over the slip, this time climbing the rice paddies above us. The terraces rose up and up through the greenery towards the bright, azure blue sky. Almost immediately, the boys divested me of my day back and physically began to haul me up the embankments as my artificial hips restricted my climbing ability. With a short sharp pain as I was being lifted by the left arm, I suddenly realised that a previously forming bone spur had broken free from my shoulder. The momentary discomfort was replaced by the freedom of movement that I could now experience.

Moving up the differing levels, we stepped carefully between the bean plants bordering each paddy. Suddenly the boys all began shouting and jumping from foot to foot. Frantically they were pointing at the ground. They were all trying to move away which was difficult as they kept changing feet. "Snake!" was the cry. Being the typical Aussies that we are, Mike and I pushed forward. And we were confronted with something looking like an earth worm. This was a young pit viper. It was searching for a way out. Twisting and turning, it tried to hide in one of the rock walls. Shepherding us away from this deadly creature, the boys insisted with continuing the climb. Kanchha had gone ahead with Kim and was following her lead to find the path descending to the trail below, laughing as they balanced on the paddy walls and skirted the carefully planted vegetables. All in all the diversion had added another 45 minutes to our day.

As I collapsed in a heap, I garnered some interest from the porters which turned out to be them alerting me to leeches. The giveaway was some tiny wrigglers on my shoes and the tell-tale spots of blood on my socks. I hit the record that morning that was not beaten on the entire trip. Between two ankles I had 13 bites that bled profusely but without pain. Dorje helped me divest my ankles of freeloaders.

Back on the trail again, the group had to climb over some minor slips but there were no incidents. It's fascinating to watch the locals when it comes to landslides. Within an hour, they will usually have forged a new path to replace the one swept away. By sheer force of numbers, the path quickly became well packed and appeared to have always been there. At times you would be walking the valley when the sound of an explosion would ricochet off the hills. Road crews are constantly repairing and attempting to build roads. Between the steep hillsides, the rain, the mountains yearly increasing in height and the occasional earthquake, road construction is a slow and laborious job.

Image: Kim Stanley-Eyles

We climbed a path along the side of a cliff with a drop of 200-300 metres but no handrails. Even when hand rails existed, they are often battered and bent by large jagged rocks tumbling from above. At one point we took a break after a particularly steep climb. We could see all the way back to Bahundanda. Dorje said that we would need to climb up before stopping for lunch. Inevitably we asked if the climb was 'Aussie up' or 'Nepali up' and Dorje replied "Oh, not flat here" at which we all laughed if somewhat nervously. The term 'Nepali up' is not to be taken lightly.

We stopped at Syange (1,100 metres) to eat lunch and stayed for about an hour and a half. Lunch stops often included sleep time. Departing at 13:30, we were heading for Jagat. As we approached Jitai, another explosion was heard followed by its long rumble. A plume of dust rose up from beyond the next bend in the valley. Soldiers stopped our progress and advised that they were blasting to clear the road. Waiting for the next firing, we encountered the disconnection between sound and light. Often the column of dust would be seen seconds before the sound reached our ears.

Not having heard the all clear, we nervously watched some locals head out on the trail. Shouldering our bags and passing some Muscovy ducks wallowing happily in a puddle, the team joined the drawn out line of locals heading up the path.

I should say at this point that I suffer from vertigo and my fear of heights was so bad that when driving, I would normally drive in the lane closest to the centre of any bridge just in case something went wrong. Nepal would teach me to face that fear and defeat it.

At the time, I noted in my journal that things became harder as we climbed up and discovered we too would have to traverse a new landslide. Large rocks were still tumbling from above. The ground, mostly broken shale, was loose under foot. Dropping down to the river, it was possibly 200 metres or more to the flooded river with no chance of stopping the slide. The path was, at times, only 20 centimetres wide. Single file was the only way to go. Mike and Kanchha were in front of Dorje and I. The girls were bringing up the rear. My heart rate monitor began to beep as I passed the alert threshold.

Dorje said we were going across so I stuck to his heels like glue. At one point, he yelled "Stop!" and put an arm in my way. A large boulder about the size of two soccer balls bounced, skipped and slid past us before eventually tumbling into the river far below. The monitor began beeping in earnest as I passed the warning threshold.

Image: Kim Stanley-Eyles

Once it was past, Dorje's diminutive hand snaked into the shoulder strap of my day back and literally dragged me forward. I was feeling exhilarated by the whole experience. Here was I dealing with my fear of heights. Then it all turned sour when a pedestrian jam stopped all movement. Walking across a steep slope without a horizon was hard enough but stopped in the middle of it all, my vertigo began to kick in. I felt the panic rising and I yelled for people to keep moving. My equilibrium was going and I began to lean outwards as my brain tried to ensure I was standing perpendicular to the ground. At the last second, the line of people moved and again Dorje grabbed my pack and led me off the landslide.

To this day, I am convinced that Dorje saved my life several times right there. My heart rate had climbed to almost 200 beats per minute during the whole experience and I had the jitters. Light headed, the whole planet seemed to be spinning around me. I wanted to collapse in a heap and run backwards and forwards across the landslide in defiance of its power at the same time. Either I was cured of my fears or driven to madness with exhilaration. Every breath brought my heart rate back down and I felt wildly alive. Colours seemed more intense and I could hear the water boiling around boulders in the river far below.

We took a break on the far side while the last of the group crossed safely. While waiting, Kanchha decided to clean the mud off Mike's backpack using wild marijuana leaves growing beside the path. Here the plants are so extensive that even on my map, they are listed as "Fields of Marijuana" although I was told it's not of smoking grade. More likely it is suitable for hemp cloth production. We did have a good laugh about what the sniffer dogs might think at the airport, and told Mike that he was going to go through customs all on his own.

The path then began a gentle decline to the village of Jagat (1,300 metres). With the approach of the afternoon thunderstorm and after a little debate, we elected to stay here. The weather gave us no choice as a distinct rumble of thunder rolled around the hills. Given that the trekking season has barely started, we could have the pick of most establishments. We chose the aptly named Eco Home Lodge. While Dorje negotiated prices, we discovered the hard way how much preparation is done just before trekking season starts when several members leant against a chair only to be told it had just been painted that afternoon. The rooms were quite comfortable and the toilets had seats rather than being squats. Little did we suspect that this porcelain throne would be the last one we would see for days. Luxury, although they still needed a bucket of water put down them to flush. Washing and toilet facilities with in an ensuite and even the plumbing nailed to the walls did not detract from the extravagance of it all. However, due to the overcast day, there wasn't a lot of solar hot water.

From our room, the view was dominated by the sheer vertical sides of the valley so close that we could almost touch them. A power line ran past the window strung from tree to tree. Up slope, a series of new concrete power poles was standing. The power lines not yet fitted. Thick lush vegetation surrounded the village. In the forecourt of the lodge was a building set with its door open, full to the doorway with corn hanging from the rafters.

Down stairs in the dining room, Mike and I shared a beer. Sandra completed her day's notes and Kim taught the boys how to play a fast paced card game called 'Spit.' Dorje and Kanchha quickly became very good at this game, although Kanchha would cheat outrageously feigning misunderstanding of the rules; the look of wide-eyed innocence betrayed by his laughter at being caught. The amount of hilarity and general merriment brought a few of the locals who shyly stood in the door way. While they may not have understood the game, the fun being had did bring out some toothy grins.

At one point in the evening, Dorje brought me an older gentleman with a fever and an infected tooth that appeared to be well on the way to abscessing. He was in quite some pain from the look in his eyes. The Nepali people are incredibly stoic when it comes to pain. With strict instructions for its use, I gave him some of our precious paracetamol and advised him to visit the dentist. Again from the look in his eye, I could tell it was a task he did not relish.

During the day, we had seen Tibetan wild cats that were choosing to share with humans. As Kim and the boys played 'Spit', a wild cat brought its kittens into the dining room. She allowed us to play with them while she obviously took a break from parenting. Keeping a motherly eye on us the whole time, the spotted tabby kittens rolled, tumbled and chomped on any fingers nearby. She even allowed us to pick them up although she was always just a claws length away.

On the recommendation of Dorje, I tried the garlic soup for the first time. It is said that this strong but flavoursome soup assists in acclimatising and helps stave off altitude sickness. It would become a mainstay of our diet until we had crested the Thorung La Pass and each village seemed to have its own recipe. I would take several years to finally locate a recipe that was close to this potent but delicious soup. However be wary of the eight or more cloves of garlic per bowl. Jyoti Pandey-Pathak, author of '*Taste of Nepal*' and now an acquaintance, advised me that it should not be consumed by those with high blood pressure or for extended periods in hot weather.

It has been a tradition with Mike and Margaret when trekking that a small Rotary-type group be formed out of the trekkers. We became known as the Thorung La Five. We had a President, Mike, a Secretary, Sandra, and a Treasurer, Margaret, who would be responsible for collecting all the 'fines' we might incur. Fines would primarily consist of a penalty of 100 rupees any time someone left an item behind that the boys had to retrieve. At the end of the trek, the collected fines (this would turn out to be quite substantial) would be given to the boys as a bonus for their hard work. Kim became Community Liaison, and I was the First Aid Officer.

Chapter 5 - A bit more up

"Travel is more than the seeing of sights; it is a change that goes on, deep and permanent, in the ideas of living." – Miriam Beard

Day four (September 10th) saw us leave Jagat between 07:30 and 08:00. We knew that some of the climbs would be steep. Not long out of the village we hit the first tough climb with an angle so steep it could have been vertical. Mike found a micro-hydro power station in a small shed next to a small waterfall. It hummed quietly to itself, indifferent to our interest and cameras.

Our climb ended with our arrival in Chamje (1,430 metres). Mike and I chatted with some friendly labourers who were hand-flattening a section of the new road that will eventually make its way up to Manang. A traffic jam of pedestrians appeared in front of us in the village. The army had closed the trail while blasting was occurring. I spoke with one friendly soldier who explained in broken English it would be quite some time before we could continue.

We settled in to wait at a tea house and had an early lunch. We had a two and a half hour wait so some time was spent sleeping or playing 'Spit.' Nearby, an unexpected sound began as someone used a hand held electric planer on some timber. The traffic jam of people now extended back past us through the village. It was amazing how many pedestrians were using the path on this day.

Our hosts decided to provide us with entertainment and turned on the satellite TV. The movie showing was "*Mortal Kombat*" with Hindi subtitles. When that finished, we were treated to a much pirated DVD of a Bollywood film called "*Luck*." Sadly the sound was out of sync with the vision. With one of the pieces of music playing Kim, Sandra, and I began dancing and were joined in short order by Dorje, Kanchha, Dhan and La Har. There was a lot of laughter as the music finished and the film continued. It was a good way to ease the waiting.

With the road opened, we walked on and crossed the Marsyangdi Nadi on a steel suspension bridge to the eastern bank. Happy with myself, I managed to cross the bridge without using my hands. My confidence was growing as my fear of heights began to ease. We watched the labourers on the other bank pushing boulders off the blasting area into the river some 200-300 metres below. A team of six pushed a rock about the size of a bus over the edge and we watched it splash heavily into the river.

The path became steep with the vegetation close to the trail on both sides. By this stage we knew that we would most likely be stopping at Tal in the late afternoon. On the other side of the river, bisecting two mountains between 4,000 and 5,000 metres, the waters of the Myardi Khola roared through a narrow cut in the rock before falling to join the Marsyangdi Nadi. In front of us rose the steep trail, full of switch backs to the saddle which marked the boundary between Lamjung and Manang provinces. This was one of the hardest climbs I would face. I really felt I was about to 'burst a boiler.' A local porter, the heavy load on his back covered by a large bright blue plastic bag against the afternoon showers, would walk short distances before resting a few minutes. By this stage the boys had taught me 'bisari bisari' which translates as 'slowly slowly.'

Eventually we crested the saddle and were greeted with the view of the plateau valley and some flat ground to travel on. Discretely tucked amongst the low scrub, an army encampment watched over the district boundary. Below us the river spread across flat wide ground giving no indication of its power before it tumbled into valley below. On its banks sat the town of Tal (1,700 metres) which also means lake. Apparently the town sometimes floods unexpectedly and the locals run to climb the steep mountains beside the village to escape. We could see where some buildings had flood damage that hadn't been repaired and white washed yet, and evidence of scouring in the riverbanks. We were probably standing at around 2,000 metres and still had to climb up some more stairs. They clung to the sides of the cliff with a battered hand rail. Reaching a point almost directly over the town, they began a series of switchbacks down to the level of the river.

Hitting flat ground, we gently walked into town and stopped for the night at our lodge. The valley was already deep in shadow. In the distance to the north was Kangaru Himal (6,981 metres); the sun illuminating its western flank. The air was beginning to chill as we settled in. The climb for the day was only 400 metres and the walk a mere nine kilometres but we had set out over eight hours ago with some extended delays in the morning.

Our stop for the night was the Tilicho Hotel and Restaurant. It was a brightly coloured two-storey affair in purple, pale yellow and multiple hues of pink with the typical narrow stairways. We washed up before the evening meal. The woman who ran the lodge served us char grilled corn which was hot and tasty. Tal was the first place we had come cross on the trek that had Annapurna Conservation Area Project (ACAP) safe drinking water. This had been set up by ACAP for the local women to earn an income by selling treated water to visiting trekkers for NPR35 per litre.

They started calling Kim 'Crunchy' which caused some confusion until they admitted it was actually "Krancie" (spelling?) which apparently means youngest sister. This made Kim's day. They apparently had been impressed by Kim's ability to keep up with them. Margaret and I had picked up colds along the way and had to travel slowly. Bed time was 19:30 and we were out like a light almost instantly.

Before the morning sunlight had fallen upon the town of Tal, we had already begun to drag ourselves out of bed. I remember at the time feeling that maybe I had not done enough psychological preparation. My greater enemy was my brain rather than my body, not that my body didn't hurt. Oh it did that. But the difficulty came in not being able to sleep. During the night, a fight had broken out between two of the Tibetan Mastiffs which had taken some time to quell.

The imperceptibly thinner air was already taking its toll on our sleeping patterns. Sandra, Kanchha, La Har and I were all feeling sick; the group a chorus of coughing.

Yet we still walked on. There was no option as we were already about a day behind. To our right a graceful waterfall tumbled from the mountain above. Perhaps next time we can take the time to visit it.

Along the path, crops grew on both banks of the river. Thick stands of corn waved in the breeze. The boys explained that this was bear country. Being as big as a water buffalo meant that there was not a lot they were afraid of so crops were often set up with trip wires leading to shotguns loaded with blanks. Somewhere above us tigers lurked in the nearby mountain, waiting for dark so that they could raid the goats. Taking a break, a puppy and a full grown mastiff played a game of 'chasey' for our amusement. The puppy was yipping with all its mighty authority and the mastiff was jumping around like a dog half its weight. Their game was a serious training session for the years to come when protecting the homes from bear and tiger would become a lifelong job.

Our party began to stretch out in a line along the trail. As we rose up beside the face of a cliff, Dorje pointed high above us where white-faced monkeys could be seen dangling over the side hunting for food. As quickly as they appeared, they were gone, my video camera still attempting to warm up, the opportunity lost. The constant rumble of the river on our left was a deep mocking laughter to my lack of planning about where the camera should sit in easy reach.

Near Khotro (1,850 metres) we stopped while a donkey train traversed the suspension bridge. Mike, Margaret and Sandra were already over while Kim and I were forced to wait. Behind the others another landslide cut an angry scar into the hillside. We walked another series of switchbacks as the sun pushed down on the western side of the river. Things began to heat up a little.

We stopped at an unoccupied building for a rest. On its roof, a tiny solar panel had been installed to run a light inside the building when it was occupied. As I picked up my day pack, a shoulder strap gave way. Mike offered to fix it there and then. Pulling from his pack a small wooden cylinder, he opened it to reveal a complete sewing kit including a length of waxed thread. The boys were fascinated as Mike showed them the double cobblers stitch.

I looked down to the river below where a huge rock, perhaps the equivalent of a two-storey house lay in the water. The scree around it suggested that it was a recent addition to the shoreline.

With my pack repaired, we were underway again. Around the next corner we were confronted with a dreadful sight. Laxmi Hotel, a trekking lodge, was completely destroyed. All around the evidence of a landslide explained the state it was in. The boulder had come down the mountain but by a fluke of geography, it had been turned on an embankment directing its full force on the lodge. Debris was everywhere. A thong half poked out of the gravel and scree. Apparently two people had been tragically killed on the site.

Not long after, I began to struggle physically again. We arrived at Dharapani (1,860 metres) and I was exhausted. The boys negotiated with the owner of Hotel Eco Himalaya & Restaurant for us to sleep on the chairs. I ended up sleeping for one and a half hours. Afterwards I felt I could face a meal which put me in better spirits.

The kitchen was basic but neatly kept. A large clay-topped table supported a wood fire that was being used for cooking. On the floor beside it, two gas burners were also being used.

Outside, the boys had scratched out a game board on a large flat stone. Smaller stones had been collected as playing pieces. It looked familiar to me but I could not place it at the time. A check with a friend in Australia identified the game as a variation sometimes known as Alquerque. This game has been tracked back over 4,000 years to Egypt and makes appearances across Europe and the Middle East in various forms.

Image: Kim Stanley-Eyles

We departed again with a promise from Dorje that we would have only a "little bit up, little bit down" although the meaning of "a little bit" varies greatly between Australia and Nepal. My legs had begun to complain; my lungs gasped for air. Mentally I was already considering giving up. But I knew going back was a) difficult at best, given the landslides and b) giving in prematurely when getting to the pass would make it all worthwhile. Kim kept up a constant chatter of encouragement to keep me going.

At one point the journey was lightened when I spotted a local squirrel zip across our path. And we saw a team of timber cutters using a manual pit saw to shape boards straight off the log.

By the time we hit Danakyu (2,300 metres) we had covered ten kilometres in just over eight hours and had climbed 600 vertical metres. We were now officially higher than anywhere on the Australian continent. Mt Kosciusko is only 2,228 metres above sea level. Our accommodation was in the two-storey Himalayan Guest House and Restaurant.

We were now beginning to encounter and recognise the same groups of travellers. Sadly some of them had no respect for local customs. One girl, wearing nothing but a small towel on the first floor balcony, wandered from one shower to the next using all of the hot water for herself. Embarrassed and disgusted locals gathered in the front courtyard to tut-tut this girl who was oblivious to the offence she was causing. There is information everywhere, including on the back of menus, explaining basic courtesy and behaviour to avoid offending the local communities.

This included such things as wearing short clothes and showing too much leg (men and women alike) as well as public shows of affection between couples which is also frowned upon. Such disrespectful actions also meant that we were forced to shower or wash in cold water. Not a pleasant experience after a long day on the trail, I can tell you, but certainly bracing.

Day six, September 12th, the weather was overcast if mild and ideal for trekking. We were now walking in a westerly direction. The path weaved around thickets of trees and was really well maintained. With a cool breeze behind us, we crossed a steel bridge where we were the confronted with our first climb of the day. Tall trees kept the sun off us initially but it was the humidity which gave us most trouble. It was difficult to lose body heat. My day pack was fitted with a two litre bladder and I carried two one-litre bottles in the side pouches. A necessary, if somewhat inconvenient weight, this water sloshed around occasionally causing me to swing from side to side. Both Margaret and I took a long time to complete the climb. The boys took advantage of the delay as they were feeling sick too. As an added bonus, they would try to find interesting plants and flowers for Margaret to photograph. It actually became a welcome diversion who could find the most exotic flower or fern. The porters were embarrassed that they were sick, and we were all looking for excuses to slow the walk down to allow time to recover. But we could not stop for long.

In between the trees we were afforded magnificent views back down the valley. Each stop we made presented us with a clear view uninhibited by smog or haze. The air was fresh with clean vegetation, the humus rich in the damp, shaded areas.

As we crested the rise, we found everyone else stretched out in the sun having a rest beside two stone and timber buildings. Along the Annapurna trail, most places had stone paved areas about the right height to rest your pack upon. They provide a great seat or at least a way to remove your pack without having to lower it to the ground. It seems a great deal of effort goes into placing these seats where you can be afforded an often magnificent view of the surrounding hills and were used by trekkers and porters carrying goods.

Under a peaked, thatched roof shelter Mike was talking with the family of a young boy who had been vomiting and suffering diarrhoea. We raided our supplies for some medication and Mike, working through the boys as interpreters, gave strict instructions on its use.

Just as we were preparing to leave, an older man approached us limping. It seemed that he had dropped some heavy wood on his foot. As far as we could determine, it had happened nearly three weeks previously.

It appeared that at some time in the past another person had 'released the pressure' but it still hurt.

We were unable to determine what 'released the pressure' actually meant but we suspected that someone may have lanced the injury. Given the stoicism of the Nepali people, for him to complain of pain, it must have been extremely sore. Kim and I inspected the injury and after asking a few questions, we suspected the toe to be quite broken. Since he kept trying to walk on the foot, it would keep moving the break, delaying the healing. We could only advise that he stay off the foot for a few days. Since this was most likely to have been ignored, we recommended that he sleep with the foot raised on a pillow to try and reduce the pressure.

Commencing a slightly gentler climb, shortly we came to the village of Timang (2,270 metres) where we took a tea break. Sandra had found a couple of little girls and a tiny boy in camouflage pants. She was entertaining them and handing out tiny stickers and balloons. They caused a fair amount of amusement when the kids discovered that they could make sounds by releasing the air from the balloons. In the shade of a little courtyard beside the trail, the girls found our two toy bears and were immediately fascinated. We let them play with the bears on the understanding that we would be taking them with us. Both Splinter and Bo, their professional names, had a specific purpose. They would be going to Thorung La Pass for photographs. The girls played like any other children, making the bears dance and sing, and even have an argument and a fight.

Dorje explained that this village had a first aid post. He said he would try and locate those who were trained to run it. A short time later, he returned with two inquisitive women. We offered to donate a first aid bundle for their supplies. Kim, with the help of Dorje, explained the various items in our bundles. They in turn produced their first aid bag. It was a professional looking bag supplied by the Red Cross Society of Nepal. On inspection, it was found to be almost completely empty. There was a face washer, a triangular bandage, a plastic bag and a lot of empty space. We agreed to leave them two bundles which they quickly transferred to the kit. While the kit had been supplied fully stocked, over time it had become depleted and due to circumstances had never been restocked. Mike gave them a lesson on the importance of hygiene and how best to sterilise the shears and scissors. Despite the overhead glaring sun, we took some pictures with the girls before departing along the trail.

By this stage, I was suffering a minor upset stomach and was beginning to look for a rest break. Sometime later we arrived at Thanchowk (2,570 metres) where we stopped for lunch. The ground here had begun to level out and we were travelling at a fair pace. The village was surrounded by fields cut into the hillsides. From our lunch stop, we could look back over the crops to the houses. Again we slept; I most heavily of all. Waking a bit woolly-headed, I was able to down a small amount of food but I really didn't feel like much.

The environment had really changed by now. The jungle conditions were long behind us, as were the daily storms. Trees grew straight and tall. Redwoods and conifers looked at odds to the steeply sloping hills, clinging tentatively in the rocky soil. This was red panda country, although we unfortunately didn't see any evidence of them. From time to time, we would pass the roadside encampments of timber cutters. Their pit saws were sometimes left abandoned while they took meals. Piles of fresh sawn boards and posts were set out ready for porters to carry to their final destination. Mike and Kanchha took a turn using the giant saw. We passed a porter who was carrying five posts each about two metres in length. He used a headband to support the load and moved slowly under the extreme weight.

Because the ground had levelled out somewhat, our walk into Chame (2,670 metres) was fairly leisurely and by the time we arrived, we were all very tired. A large boulder was painted in English and Devangari. "Broadband Internet Now in Chame" it proclaimed. A broad road led into the town under a large wooden and stonework archway. Our accommodations at the Hotel Marsyangdi Mandala were chalet style huts with thicker mattresses and pillows, painted in the common blue and pink trim of the Tibetan influence.

Image: Margaret Evans

Each room had power points. Around each chalet, a lush garden grew; large blooms adding to the profusion of colour. The day had been relatively short at around five hours but we had covered about 11 kilometres and climbed around 470 metres. We were all glad to find ample hot water for showers. Sandra enjoyed garlic soup and steamed vegetable momos. If I remember rightly, I probably had an omelette. One of the few dishes I could regularly face along with the garlic soup. Mike and Kim hadn't lost their appetites and had settled in with their regular fried rice with egg and garlic soup. Kim had decided to try the garlic soup at every dinner to compare recipes.

Unsure how long the internet cafe would be open, I wolfed down some food and walked back to check it out. I discovered that it was open but learnt the hard way how expensive it could be. At the BPD Monastery, the fee was 60 rupees an hour ($AU0.70) while my hour and a half in Chame ended up costing me around $AU15.00. Incredibly expensive, I now knew I should pre-type my blog entries and cut and paste the posts.

Another surprising discovery was my mobile phone began ringing. Kate had managed to get my phone provider to reactivate global roaming. With my eyes feeling like they would fall out of my head, I returned to the cabin where I quickly fell asleep to the rumble of the mighty river below us.

I woke ridiculously early the next morning and lay listening to music until the traces of morning light crept down into the valley. Kim had a rough night as the bed was too hard for her and her hips and lower back were sore. Being too tired the night before, I had not paid much attention to the landscape around us. This morning, however, was a completely different story. Rising steeply above us, three snow-cloaked peaks sat sentinel like around us. To the west rose Annapurna II (7,937 metres), to the south Lamjung Himal (6,983 metres) and to the north Kangaru Himal (6,981 metres). The bright sun light and pale blue sky sharply outlined the mountains around us.

With sunny, clear but chilly air, we again hit the trail. The air was thinner making climbing harder. Frequent rest stops allowed us to take in the magnificent views surrounding us. At times the climb was quite gentle as we passed through forests that Mike and Margaret equated to the ones they had seen in Montana. Again we were reminded that we were in bear and tiger country but we remained disappointed by the shy creatures. A magnificent woodpecker stopped us in our tracks for about five minutes as it foraged on the path in front of us.

During our walk through the forest, the fast jingle of a bell announced the approach of a donkey in the opposite direction. On its back sat a haughty looking monk in burgundy robes. Overhead we heard the sound of a helicopter heading south; possibly a rescue flight removing some trekker in trouble or a VIP being flown around by the government. Heading back down the trail, a man approached us and waved us to stop. Dorje stepped forward to talk with him and was handed a letter in a plastic pocket. The letter was from a doctor listing all the diseases the man had, including typhoid and requesting any assistance. A separate sheet was included so that donors could write their details. Dorje handed the man 100 rupees and we walked on.

Image: Kim Stanley-Eyles

Leaving the forest behind, the road rose and fell until we had climbed and were walking along the face of a cliff. The path had been blasted into an undercut during construction; the sheer rock face rising above us. At one place, possibly Bhratang, we passed to the left of a long line of prayer wheels at the base of which were some Mani stones. These stones are each carved with the mantra "Om Mani Padme Hum" which loosely translates as "Hail to the jewel in the lotus" and is created as a form of devotion.

Lunch was at Dhikur Pokhari (3,060 metres) where we enjoyed the view in the warming sun. A cool breeze gently blew around us without being cold. On the deck in front of the restaurant, Mike lay down on the timbers while Margaret walked up and down his back. North of the river, Swargadwari Dande rose over 1,000 metres in height following a great sweeping curve to the east and over six kilometres long. For those who have been to Victoria, it left the Elephants Hide in the Grampians for dead. In the quiet, clear air, voices could be clearly heard over two kilometres away across the valley. One of the porters, Dhan I think, spotted people well up the steep sides. It took a few more minutes to locate them with the zoom lens on the video camera. We soon found a group of wild garlic harvesters with large cane baskets on their backs. Staying on the extremely steep slope for several days at a time they would fill their baskets with these delicacies and bring them down to sell at local markets. At the tea-house, on the ever present stone shelf, a mountain bike rested. Instead of being ridden, it was being carried up the steep slopes.

Each night we would try and rinse out our clothes. They would be hung out overnight but invariably they would still be damp in the morning. As a result, our backpacks became walking clothes lines. During our stop for lunch today, the clothes were laid out on the boards in the sun and by the time we departed, they were mostly dry.

The final stretch to Lower Pisang (3,200 metres) should have taken 45 minutes by Dorje's reckoning but it was just over an hour before we finally arrived. We approached over a wooden bridge and through another timber and stone archway. On the outskirts of the town, a building proudly displayed both a vulture and a yak that had been preserved in the manner of taxidermy. The vulture was hanging under the eaves to look like it was flying.

Lower Pisang is the more modern town catering to trekkers in the area. Houses are a combination of stone and timber. The roofing boards covered in stones to hold them in place. Nails are a rarity up here. The stones do a better job of holding the roofs in place during the wind storms that can blow down the valleys at this altitude, and are more easily replaced. Upper Pisang overlooks it but is more medieval in its aspect and supports a monastery. At evening and morning time, the sounds of voice and drum would drift down to us. In the chilling night air, the smoke from its fires drifted down the slope, hugging the ground as it moved.

Again our cabins were snug and comfortable. The walls were simple ply board sheets but behind them was a layer of the black foam sometimes used inside speaker cabinets. Unfortunately we were restricted to a bucket wash as one of the other travelling groups had managed to use all the water. The dining room of the Everest Guesthouse gave a wide view across to the northern side of the valley. A small wood fire sat in the middle room mounted on a base of dried clay. In the corner of the room, near the kitchen, on a raised platform was a small TV before a floor rug. From the kitchen drifted the sounds of Celine Dion. Mike read a book, sharing a beer with me while Sandra completed her journal and Kim played a game of solitaire. Margaret was resting in her room. The boys were off socialising. We had climbed around 500 metres over a distance of about 18 kilometres.

After the evening meal, when the power was back on, locals began drifting in to watch a movie on the TV. It turned out to be "*Resident Evil 3*" which grabbed Kim's attention. She sat with them laughing at the gore while the others recoiled in fascinated horror. I retreated to our room and was fast asleep.

Sandra woke during the night to the sounds of nibbling in her room. She was not quick enough to switch on a light/torch and actually see what it was, but there was evidence there had been something enjoying 'treats' from her backpack. Our rooms were definitely not rodent proof.

Chapter 6 - To Manang and beyond: The run to Thorung Pedi

"Too often... I would hear men boast of the miles covered that day, rarely of what they had seen." – Louis L'Amour

On our 8th day on the trail, we were heading for Manang and our two-day acclimatisation stop. We would cover around 16 kilometres and climb 290 metres by the time we were done. My sleep the previous night had been interrupted. We were in the Altitude Sickness zone. Some of the mild symptoms include disturbed sleep patterns, fatigue during exertion, headache and suppressed appetite.

Sandra reported slight nose bleeds; not really bleeding, just blood on her hanky when she wiped her nose. She had her first experience of this at Chame. It became the norm for her.

But despite the wake/sleep pattern of the previous night, I awoke feeling good. The morning was chilly and the sky bright blue. The nights had become cold enough that extra layers were required but the days were pleasantly warm. Thank goodness we had heeded the advice to dress in layers as it meant they could be removed as the temperature grew warmer.

The morning's views were of Chulu East (6,429 metres) and Annapurna II. I managed to face a breakfast of apple porridge although I wasn't too enthusiastic. Something about the effects of the altitude managed to remove my desire to eat. As part of our normal routine, we obtained boiled water to restock our drinking supplies. By this point on the trail, we were starting to encounter regular safe water stations.

Setup by the government and run by the local villages, the stations use ozone filtration systems. Income from the sales of this clean, cold drinking water is invested back into the village. This early on the trail, a litre cost about $AU0.60 although the price would rise the further we went. The best part of this system is that the water requires no further treatment and can be drunk straight away with no after taste.

With a gentle breeze blowing in the glorious sunlight, we began a steady climb. The trees started to thin out and the ground became rockier. Sandra, Margaret and I were beginning to breathe much harder in the thinner air. Eventually we broke out at a viewpoint at Deuralidanda (3,486 metres) where Dorje talked about one of the climbs he had done when he was younger. When asked about how old he was now, he replied that he was 28. Margaret laughed and claimed that Dorje had been 28 for several years already to which he replied with a slight grin. He pointed toward the northwest to a stepped peak known as Chulu West (6,419 metres) and explained how during that climb, the mountaineers had worked through the night to get near their goal before making the final push on the summit. He had been unable to complete the climb and had rested on a plateau below the summit waiting for the climbers to return. As he related his story Mike climbed up slightly higher again so that he could capture footage of the view and of us. It was here that we first met up with a group of younger English lads on their gap year. They were a friendly bunch although it would be days before we really got to talking. They were determined to make the trip in half the recommended time so that they could indulge in side-trips. They were practically running up the mountains.

From here we could see straight up the valley towards Humde, Bhraka and Manang; the ground ahead looking relatively flat. Flowing clouds hid a series of the other peaks but did little to cast shadows. The temperature was warm but comfortable.

We began an easy descent (at last, a little bit of down) into the broad meadow-like valley. The ground here was relatively flat and the vegetation now quite a bit shorter. The river was no longer the imposing thing it had been earlier in the trek. In fact it could no longer be heard as a constant rumble. Hitting the flat ground we all began to stride off and our line began to string out. We passed an unloaded donkey train heading in the opposite direction. The road was wide and flat as we walked along, passing vacant and sometimes partially collapsed structures. The boys explained that these are used by yak herders during winter. This area can receive deep snow but normally the area is good for winter pastures. Each structure is the equivalent of stables. Despite looking run down, the herders will repair and rebuild them as their charges move into the area.

More timber cutters worked in this valley and we saw shaped beams being carried up to Manang again by porter power, the beams often exceeding three metres in length. Having put some distance on the rest of the group, Kim and I took a short break. We looked down on the much diminished Marsyangdi Nadi as it cut into the valley floor. The light here was bright, intensified by the reflection of the stark white ground. We were buffeted by the increasing westerly winds. Everyone else caught up and we found out that they had stopped at a little curio store selling local gifts that we had seen but chosen to ignore. The others had chosen to stop because they were intrigued by the sign "Local Antiques". Although they were not sure there were really any true antiques there.

Moving on, we headed for Humde (3,280 metres) for a tea stop. Humde contains the last air strip on the eastern side of the pass. As we entered the town, we passed one of the more unusual things you might find in Nepal, a German-style bakery. Already trekkers were lining up to buy bread; freshly baked that day but quickly becoming stale in the dry air. Closer to the airport, we stopped for a cup of tea. Noisy voices behind a dried mud wall turned out to be some labourers collecting potatoes from a field beside the airport fence. The day already having felt like such an easy pace and relaxing in the sun, we had to remain mindful of how quickly you can become sunburnt. It was much quicker at this altitude and with greater effect. But it was still tempting just to lie down and sleep in the warming sun. The thinner air made it harder to breath and my feet were feeling like blocks of concrete.

113

With a sigh, I loaded up my day pack as we began to head out along the trail. A little up, a little down and we covered the next six kilometres fairly quickly. Approaching a steel bridge over the river, I met a gentleman who spoke very good English. He had just retired and was on his way walking to Kathmandu to petition for his pension. Very few people actually get pensions although teachers do. It would take him eight days to get there, and then more to go through the petition process.

Entering the ancient village of Bhraka (3,360 metres), we stopped at Hotel New Yak. This name along with many others showed the great sense of humour that is a hallmark of the Nepali. From the main room of the hotel we gazed up at the majestic Annapurna III (7,555 metres) and Ganggapurna (7,454 metres) to the south west and Annapurna IV (7,525 metres) to the south east. To the north rose the Kangla Himal range. Our menu included yak for the first time but we weren't up to a big meal yet.

Image: Sandra Gormley

It was here, on the bright sunny hotel balcony, that we tried Sea-buckthorn juice for the very first time. Distinctive to this area of Nepal, the tiny, astringent berries of the willow-leaved sea-buckthorn are harvested by local women and blended with water and honey into a surprisingly sweet, thick juice with hinted overtones of apricot nectar. It has 15 times more vitamin C than oranges. The difficulty in harvesting is the removal of the berries from amongst the formidable array of thorns on each branch. A large glass (BG=big glass as written in the menu) cost NPR150 or $AU1.61 and is definitely worth the investment. As I drank it down, I could almost feel the energy coming back to me.

One of the fond memories that Mike and Margaret had shared with us from their previous visits was related to the Nepali skill in cooking chips. They have definitely mastered frying potatoes to a crispy finish. Our first experience was of a plate of crunchy, golden brown chips which were fluffy on the inside. There is something to be said for vegetables grown without poisons or chemicals.

The tiny village of Bhraka sits back from the main trail on a gently rising slope of open grassland. While we were waiting for lunch, Sandra took some time to take a series of photos. Several gorgeous young children modelled for her and one of the images served as her screen saver for the next year. Around the trail sat modern buildings focused on the tourist trade but the original buildings date back many hundreds of years. Multi-storeyed steps rise above the ground. Access to the upper levels is gained by ancient logs carved into ladders. These were drawn up if the village was attacked, effectively protecting the residents while they threw missiles from above onto the foe. It was laid out in the bright, glaring sunlight. The short grass occasionally shaded by a few hardy trees and scrubby plants in sheltered spots. The tall trees and forest long behind us A small water-powered prayer wheel operated beside the trail. The fast flowing water kept the wheel in constant motion.

More glacial in nature, the valley was wider here. Now much narrower but still powerful, the Marsyangdi Nadi flowed beside the trail, the water coloured the grey milkiness of glacial runoff. To the south amongst the eroded columns of some Himalayan salt cliffs, Milarepa's Cave could just be made out. This was the site in the 11th century where Saint Milarepa spent time meditating.

Despite the relatively flat ground and pleasant weather conditions, the next thirty minutes of walking into Manang (3,540 metres) was very hard. Entering the outskirts of the town, a sign announced our location. Another sign clearly stated in both Devangari script and images that horses were not to be ridden, but walked within the town boundaries. An explanatory note identified that snow leopards and musk deer were present in the area. "Annapurna Highvision Hall" proudly announced that they had a projector. Local films were shown at this cinema particularly during the trekking seasons.

Drifting into Manang, we located another Tilicho Hotel and Restaurant, which was no relation to the one in Tal, and checked in. It was a very impressive lodge. The three-storey building had a central stone-paved courtyard. A bakery and coffee shop were downstairs to the right of the doorway. Nearby roofs were held in place by preformed concrete blocks or collections of stones, but here nails appeared to have been used. Solar hot water panels covered portions of the roof with many storage tanks. Several very young children, two girls and a tiny boy, immediately commenced a traditional dance in welcome. It was hard not to chuckle when one of the girls decided that the other children were obviously doing it wrong and tried to correct them while still dancing. We staggered up the narrow staircase and found our rooms. A hot shower awaited us. Sandra reminds me that the showers were communal but that the rooms had ensuite toilets.

A note at this point regarding toilets. Apart from very few exceptions, the toilet situation takes a little getting used to in Nepal. Squat toilets initially require a brave constitution, combining balancing on tired legs and careful positioning to avoid embarrassment. A bucket of water to ladle waste away is usually kept topped up by the tea house hosts during their regular cleaning, however it's the other bucket that is the real difference. It is for used toilet tissue which can clog the system. Paper is discretely taken away to be dried and then burned.

Having settled in and cleaned up, we headed further into town for some shopping. Since the trekking season had barely started, many of the shops were still not open. The majority of them were built on the south side of the path. The north side often being garden beds in front of houses set well back from the paved thoroughfare. A lot of the shops were targeted towards restocking travellers. Replacement packs, clothes and boots were for sale at prices vastly higher than would be found in Kathmandu. Strolling slowly along the path, we perused the goods without any real interest; illness and altitude working to limit our available breath.

While the others did some window-shopping, I took time to talk to a donkey (yes I talk to animals) that was wearing a traditional saddle-cloth. The work put into embroidering the material ensured that these would be heirlooms handed down for many generations, yet hard wearing enough for day to day use. The donkeys are sturdy little animals with a lovely disposition. Never did we see one mistreated and to see one lame was very rare.

Reaching the end of the shops, we turned to come back to the hotel. Sitting out the front of a single shop below a dwelling, a Tibetan woman tentatively waved in reply to our call of Namaste. The windows seemed dusty and closed in but the traditional woollen items hanging out the front drew our eyes. She was the only shop on that side of the path and could easily have been overlooked. With a couple of the boys in tow, we decided to check it out. Sandra and Kim investigated the wares. The shop was dark inside, owing to the grubby windows. In traditional clothing, she busied herself proffering various items in different colours and styles.

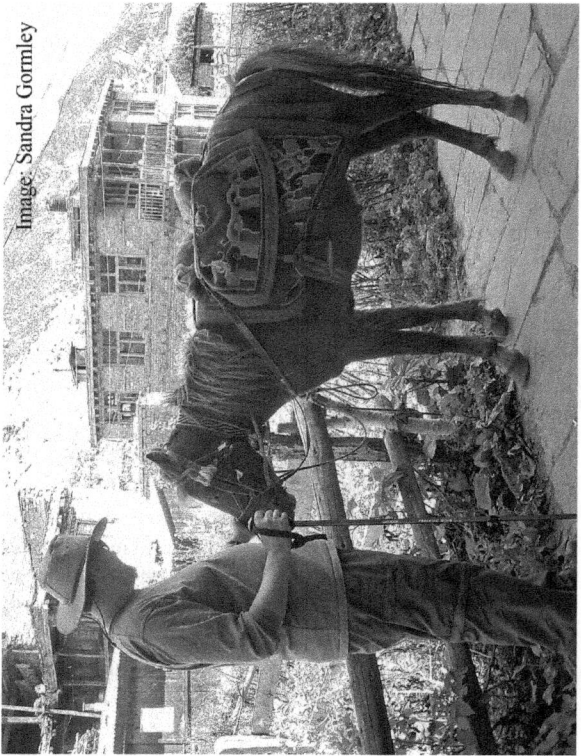

Image: Sandra Gormley

With some negotiation and haggling, a price was settled on a gorgeous purple pashmina, woven and dyed with traditional methods. Smiles and laughter between us all meant we had made a new friend.

Returning to the hotel we settled in to rest. Our extra time here in Manang was to allow us to acclimatise to the new altitude. Preparing for the climb that would be ahead of us in the next few days was an important task that could not be ignored. The normal practice is to take a full day to rest. During the day a trekker should climb up to a high point above Manang before returning to the village

Having ordered our evening meal from the hotel's restaurant, I took a punt and asked if it would be possible to see and video the kitchen. With a confused expression by the waiter, he agreed and escorted me to the kitchen. Some embarrassed chuckling from the kitchen staff accompanied my appearance in the door way but they need not have been worried. The kitchen was organised and functioning efficiently. A range of cooking methods was in use. From an open fire to LPG and hand-pumped, high pressure kerosene cookers, food was in varying states of preparation. Several pressure cookers hissed over the flames. One wall was an orderly collection of thermos jugs and various eating and drinking vessels. Freshly harvested vegetables were lined up where the 'mise en place' had been set out limiting delivery time after ordering. In the rapidly fading light, I was able to catch some of the action in the kitchen before we retreated to let them finish our orders.

The evening turned cold and the wind blew hard against the outside of the building. Even here it became dark early. Mike and I shared a beer and discussed the potential of a later trek where we would cut cross country around Lake Tilicho. It would need extra equipment, as we would be away from civilisation for a couple of days before arriving at Jomsom.

Day nine was the official acclimatisation day. Despite being the only day we could officially sleep in, I still woke at 06:30 after a restless night. Rising quietly, I left Kim to sleep and climbed onto the roof so that I could take pictures of the surrounding skyline. Mike joined me while he took some video footage. Sadly a low lying cloud or fog bank obscured most of the surrounding hills. Below me at the back of the hotel, the single-storey porters' accommodation showed some signs of life as the odd person walked in and out. To the south west between Ganggapurna and Annapurna III lay the Ganggapurna Glacier. The dirty face of the ice at well over 5,000 metres seemed to indicate that this had once been a much greater body extending well down towards the milky blue lake bearing its name far below. The air was sharp and cool without a hint of pollution. Peeking over Jong Ri (6,091 metres), the sun began its daily run across the sky.

Again food held no interest for me and I found breakfast uninteresting. My appetite was supressed in the grip of mild altitude sickness. The one thing that seemed to beat it was the glass of sea-buckthorn juice. The recommended method of improving your sleep and getting used to the altitude is to "climb high and sleep low." In other words, find a place to walk to that is higher than where you will be sleeping. For acclimatising purposes, we chose to head to Chongkor Lookout Point and a yak herder's encampment on the south side of the valley at 4,000 metres. Despite it being a day off for the boys, Dorje and Kanchha came along to assess us in our altitude adjustment. Following a trail off the main path through Manang, we descended to the level of the river and crossed on a metal bridge. A high school sat on the river flats but was surrounded by barbed wire and looked to be abandoned. On the opposite side of the river we discovered several unoccupied houses.

Our climb up from the valley floor was steep. At a fork in the path we proceeded to the west climbing to the top of a knife-edged ridge line with a sheer drop to the milky green lake far below. A fence line had been established to prevent people falling off the edge particularly when the wind was strong. Pausing for frequent stops, we laboured up the path before merging with the other path. Beginning a series of small switchbacks we eventually broke out of a stunted forest at Chongkor. It was surrounded by a stone fence which we later discovered would be used for containing the yak herds when they were down this low.

The restaurant at Chongkor had not yet opened for the season but we were able to experience the sweeping vistas of the Gungang and Kangla Himals to the north. Climbing higher we came upon the yak herders camp with its many stone pens. A temporary encampment was set up and timber cutters were working on the tree line. Despite the lack of oxygen, it was the view that was truly breathtaking. To have stayed here overnight would have allowed us to experience the ever changing beauty of the region, however with the afternoon comes very strong winds which can take you off your feet. The ever present Bo and Splinter bears again featured prominently in our photos.

Despite near exhaustion, Kim challenged Kanchha to a race to the top of a knoll with a small stone monument and they ran the last 50 metres or so. Kanchha danced to the top easily while Kim made it up almost on hands and knees, laughing and only just behind.

A local boy from the yak herder's encampment spotted the bears and became very friendly. His ultimate goal was to make off with one of them and it took all of Kim's skills in handling children to try and keep it from him. Despite the language problem, she was able to retain the bear by tickling the boy to the point he could barely move. Managing to get a grip on a leg of the bear, he did not want to let go even with the urgings of Dorje and Kanchha. Eventually the boy's father came to our rescue and with a few choice gruff words, Kim retrieved her prize. We then began our descent with a pause for an impromptu game of cricket on a relatively flat piece of ground using walking sticks as bats, and dried dung and pine cones as balls. Oddly enough it seemed harder to climb down as the hill was steep and the ground was covered in loose gravel. At one point we caught up with one of the timber cutters who was bringing down three large beams of timber on a forehead strap. He was an older man with some canvas shoes and we found him taking a break. Dorje decided to show off his own skills by lifting the load onto his head. By his reckoning, the combined weight of the timber was around 100 kilograms. Other timber cutters we encountered that day were carrying similar loads but wearing 'Crocs' instead of proper shoes. I suppose it beats doing the work in thongs. As Sandra said, "not much support on that loose track though."

Making our way back into the town, we returned to the hotel for lunch and a rest. Passing by the shop we had visited yesterday, we called out Namaste to the woman who broke out in a beautiful beaming smile. It seemed that she did not see much custom and was delighted that we had remembered her. During the afternoon, we wandered over to the office of the Himalayan Rescue Association where a talk on altitude sickness had been advertised. Even back in Besi Sahar we had seen a flyer listed on the wall. We found the building closed up tight with no signs of activity so we missed out.

Returning to the hotel, I went to the dining room in a vain attempt to transfer images from the cameras to the laptop but the power failed and so did the laptop. Its battery had not been brilliant to start with. The power did not come on again that night. While sitting drinking some tea, a lovely couple from New Zealand, judging by the accent, were eating their meal early. They had already reached dessert. With a look of chagrin, the gentleman admitted to having ordered a deep fried Mars Bar. Such decadent behaviour! It duly arrived but it was not what any of us thought it would be. The caramel confection arrived having been cooked in what looked like a thick spring roll wrapper. Australians would find the description of a Chiko Roll wrapper probably better to understand. He cut into it with his spoon and the steaming hot contents oozed onto the plate; the familiar sickly sweet scent filling the room. "I feel so dirty," was his only comment as he tucked in to the treat.

One of the most surprising things I noted on the trail was the types of products readily available at little stands along the way. For the tiniest of prices you could buy Mars Bars, Snickers, Pringles, Coca Cola, Merinda (an orange soft drink), and an assortment of lollies. These could all be found sitting side by side with cheap cigarettes and bottles of beer and spirits. There was no guarantee how far out of date the chocolate bars would actually be, but the taste of home always made it worthwhile. Here in Manang, we invested in a few Mars Bars and Snickers for a celebration once we hit the pass.

After a bland, sugar-free diet for many days, an oversweet Mars Bar doesn't have quite the same appeal as at home.

Mike and Sandra spent part of the afternoon exploring the Manang Cultural Museum. It was a traditional three storey domestic building. The animals were kept on the ground level, with a stuffed yak and different threshing machines on display. The middle storey was the storerooms, where food for the family and animals was kept to last over the winter. The upper storey was the living space. There were a huge variety of weapons, tools, utensils and clothing on display. The kitchen was the largest room where the cooking, eating and socialising happened. There was a prayer room filled with artefacts and a tiny bedroom with narrow, very hard beds. Firewood was stacked around the roof top and in the past would have deterred anyone trying to climb up and attack.

It felt unusual to go to bed and huff and puff as soon as you lay down. The power came back on about 11pm as the light outside Sandra's window came on and woke her up.

September 16th was day 10 and it saw us heading far above the tree line. It was hard walking for all of us. As we approached an archway with a centre line of prayer wheels, we were impressed by the ingenuity of the locals. As some of the old brass prayer wheels had become damaged or lost, replacements had been fashioned from Nescafe, powered milk and fruit tins roughly the same size and fitted to timber spindles. Interestingly, it was not immediately apparent that this had been done until you realised remnants of the original paper wrapper were still attached.

Image: Kim Stanley-Eyles

Entering the ancient part of Manang, our spirits did lift somewhat. The older buildings all seemed to have a defensive note to them. Tall stone walls enclosed narrow pathways with many turns in them. All perfect for spoiling attackers intentions. There were too many locations to set up ambushes and to drop things from above. Doorways were made of thick, stout wood many hundreds of years old, their surfaces worn smooth by many hands rubbing them. On many, Devangari characters were painted. To my limited understanding they appeared to be numbers and were possible part of an addressing system used in Nepal. On the thick lintel over one doorway was inscribed in poor English words, announcing that this was a "Helth Post" and bearing a red cross. The door bore the same inscription although health had been spelt correctly. There were remnants of old notices that had previously been stuck to the door. Like so many others, this was locked tight. Cool breezes flowed from the few open doorways carrying with them the scent of earth. A sure sign that the ground floors were being used for storing root vegetables like potatoes. Roofs were all flat from which sprouted vertical posts bearing upright prayer flags, their colours fluttering in the breeze.

Wandering the tight lane ways, suddenly an almost embarrassed voice came out of nowhere. It said "Namaste" and began giggling as we looked in all directions to locate the source. Eventually we realised it had come from a flat roof top above and quickly found the laughing children. We waved and called back before continuing on our way.

Coming to the outskirts of town, the path led us beside an amazing patchwork of fields thick with assorted crops. Yellowing corn swayed in the breeze beside the bright pinks of buckwheat. Large, dark green cabbages took over beds beside an open form of cauliflower.

The path began an ever insistent rise and while not particularly tough climbing for the most part, the thinner air and our 'trail cough' made it harder work than it might otherwise have been. It was not unusual for a collective coughing fit to be heard from our group as we walked along. The constant open mouthed breathing as we exerted ourselves left us more prone to picking up throat infections. I was told that this is not an uncommon experience for many trekkers.

Sandra bought a light scarf in Manang to counteract the problem but which later caused breathing difficulties once we reached higher altitudes.

We bid farewell to the Marsyangdi Nadi as it peeled off to the west from its source on the shores of Tilicho Tal. From this point we would follow the Thorung Khola and later the Kone Khola. Our morning stop was at Ghusang (3,900 metres) where we collapsed and drank tea. The air temperature was around 10 degrees so we had to break out coats and jackets. At each stop we had a selection of drinks to choose from. Do we have black tea, Nepali tea, lemon tea, masala tea, tea with lemon, mint tea or ginger tea? We had become fond of ginger and honey tea along the trip and ordered it as often as it was available, although Kim was also partial to the masala tea. Coffee was generally unavailable.

The surrounding terrain was sparsely covered with mosses, lichens, grasses and ground covers being the predominant vegetation. What shrubs were present were often low, coarse affairs with woody stems and small, tough leaves.

Ghusang is pretty much just a series of hotels and lodges for trekkers; often being closed out of season. But what passed through the village was a treat. Tied to either side of a donkey were two wheels of yak cheese. Dorje procured some for us to try. It was a lovely cheese; mild, slightly chewy and still managing to maintain a certain crumbliness to it. After days of not wanting to face food, it seemed to stimulate my taste buds.

Wandering around the grounds, Mike came face to face with an item we had previously seen but had no idea as to its purpose. Looking like a form of satellite dish but pointing towards the ground, its purpose completely stumped me. Here, we discovered they were a form of solar cooker. Pointed towards the ground when not in use, they could be rotated upward with a cooking vessel placed in the confluence of light and heat directed by the shiny surface inside. Relatively inexpensive, if somewhat time consuming, they more than compensate in savings against the use of expensive and limited timber for fires. In the middle of this one sat a large aluminium kettle.

But the trail called, so we gathered our bags and once again joined the small but determined groups of trekkers making for the pass. Our constant companions had grown so that we could regularly identify the Spanish brothers, the disparate young Israelis recently finished their terms of national service, and the two oncology nurses from New Zealand. Others drifted in and out of our circle such as the other Spanish couple who we later identified from our pictures as having passed us sitting on top of a bus on our way to Besi Sahar.

We had been teaching Dorje colloquial Australian terms which he had been trying out on other groups we briefly came across. 'Struth Ruth' soon became a favourite, and 'Stone the flamin' crows' was proving difficult to master. As we heard Australian accents coming down the path towards us from a couple travelling the circuit from the other direction, an almost perfect 'G'day mate, how's it hangin'' almost made them fall off the mountain in surprise. It turned out this nice Australian couple was suffering from tummy trouble. They didn't know about the problems with drinking the water straight from the tap and had assumed that since the water was coming from the tops of glaciers and snowy mountains that it was pristine. We told them about all the upstream villages that use the rivers as a convenient rubbish disposal, and some of the nasties that live in it. There is a reason you boil water for drinking or use the treated water services when you can find them.

The group was stringing out along the trail and we leap-frogged each other at various times. The sky was partially cloudy, a warming sun alternating with a wind already biting with the chill that would affect us on the next day. We passed a Mani wall near Karche.

Image: Mike Evans

133

At one point, puffing and huffing, we stopped at Ghyanchang. This consisted of a single hotel which had not yet opened for the trekking season. To the north east rose Chulu West, Central and East (6,419-6,584-6,429 metres respectively) outlined against the now glaring sky. Around us, the terrain rolled and yet it appeared smooth, almost like a heath land. It would have not have seemed out of place if a Scottish highland crofters hut sat in the distance with peat smoke lazily drifting from the chimney. Were it not for the deep, deep snow in winter (and the inability for us to draw a full breath), this might be a lovely place to live. As we departed, we crossed yet another steel suspension bridge above the Ghyanchang Khola.

The valley, while steep sided, actually gave us what would normally be considered a relatively gentle rising trail. However at this altitude, the going was becoming very tough. The lack of oxygen combined with a good dose of trail cough was taking its toll on our effectiveness. To break up the effort required, the boys showed us several yak herders' encampments along the way. Their keen eye picked out wild blue sheep grazing on the far side of the valley. We were duly informed that we were well into snow leopard country now but we really didn't have a hope of spotting these elusive creatures amongst scattered grey rocks and sparse grey/green scrubby plants. It did not stop us from trying and for the rest of the day, our eyes were cast upwards whenever we didn't need to watch where we were going.

When we departed from Bhulbhule, the path had often been compacted earth and grass. The higher we climbed, the more we encountered either rough stone or hand-shaped stone paths. Closer to Manang, we travelled over fine gravel tracks but anytime we climbed, the beaten earth was often broken up by rocks of assorted sizes. At lower altitudes, streams would cross the paths. Higher up the ground was dry and wind-blown.

Here above Ghyanchang, the ground we covered broke out into flat land with almost bowling green short grass. At one such point we passed a very long Mani wall. By this time, the anabatic (or Mustang) winds had really picked up driving fine grit into our faces. We each made good use of our face scarves and bandanas. Kim had managed to tie her wide-brimmed hat to her head with a large bandana that also twisted up over her mouth and nose. Sunglasses firmly tied on covered the rest of her face.

Pushing on, we eventually reached a thriving little settlement at Yak Kharka (4,018 metres) where we decided to hole up for lunch at Sainco Restaurant and Tea Shop. The building was clean, neat, bright and solid against the wind. From the first floor windows, we were able to rest and take in the views before attempting to snooze.

It had a lovely sun room, so we could take advantage of the sun without the chill of the wind. Mike had his photo taken with his trousers off and his large scarf wrapped around him like a sarong as he changed into shorts.

Fortified for the next part of the walk, we headed out into the wind again. Adequate shelter was few and far between. The path was beginning to occasionally fade away in the vegetation splitting into multiple tracks all generally heading the same direction like sheep tracks across a paddock. A series of house size square boulders appeared in front of us just as we took a break; the only windbreak to truly help us against the ever present wind. Our ten kilometre walk was nearly over for the day. After climbing around 660 metres, I finally staggered in to Ledar (4,200 metres) about an hour after everyone else.

I wondered at the time if my breathing difficulties were what industrial asthma might feel like, the fine particulate matter constantly attempting to scour our bodies and our throats. Studies I have taken in 2012 revealed that we may have been suffering a form of exercise induced asthma. The airways irritated by the constantly open mouths, the low oxygen levels, and fine dust particles in the air.

Several of the boys had jogged on ahead to confirm our accommodation. What we were not prepared for was the one true disappointment of the trip. The planned hotel had given away our rooms. Left with no alternative, Dorje booked us into Snowland Hotel and Restaurant. He seemed somewhat devastated by this turn of events. Our guide and friend was setting great store in giving us, his first customers as a solo guide, the best possible experience, and took any problems personally.

There are many inconveniences I would put up with for the joyful experience of travelling. However

Snowland was in a class of its own with a plethora of issues. The rooms seemed incomplete. Internal render was crumbling from the walls. Dados were not finished. None of the rooms had lights. Doors were almost too wide to swing past the walls on opening. Great chunks were missing from between the logs that formed the floor of the room above and some of the floor boards overhead were split lengthwise. They did not appear to be safe enough to bear weight. Sandra reported wet mattresses. She was in an underground, or so it seemed, twin room by herself and both mattresses were dripping and mouldy smelling. The floor, ceiling and walls all had a rakish way of not apparently meeting. There was no hot water and no water at all to refill the toilet flushing bucket.

While it only takes a small adjustment to get used to squat toilets, they are not built with cisterns. The user must pour water down the drain after use. Snowland had made no provision for refilling the bucket by the user. As such, after two or three users, it was not possible to flush at all and that IS as unpleasant at it sounds.

The hotel at least had a sun room which served as both a dining room and sleeping quarters for the boys. It was in this room that we ordered, and ultimately returned, our evening meals. The serves of "Chow Mein" were inedible being laden with salt and generally very poorly prepared. Sent back with a strong note of complaint, we broke out a packet of biscuits, some of our precious supply of Mars Bars, two hard-boiled eggs souvenired from lunch and some scroggin (a healthy mixture of nuts, dried fruit and white chocolate bits) that Mike had kindly donated.

The pot of ginger tea was a pot of hot water and (what appeared to be) half a tin of powdered ginger for flavouring. I suppose the pot of hot chocolate was close. There was no milk and when I went back for some, the host just kept shovelling in more drinking chocolate. At least it was drinkable.

We discovered afterwards that the wife of the owner was not present due to illness and this accounted for the inedible food and the terrible service.

Retreating to our rooms in the freezing night air, we prepared to settle in for the night. However in another case of excitement, Kim and I discovered the largest, hairiest millipede we had ever seen scurrying around the room. We lost sight of it after having filmed and soon convinced ourselves of it crawling into bed with us during the night. Kim elected to sleep with me on my single bed platform, and we put her mattress on top of mine for a little extra padding. At the beginning, the hard bed bases and thin foam mattresses where tolerable. However as we climbed and our bodies became sore, they soon became a source of great discomfort and sleepless nights. It was a very squishy night but at least we were warm.

Day 11, the following morning dawned clear, bright and exceedingly cold. Given the steep aspect of the valley, it always took some time for the sun to reach down and caress us with its warming rays. We gathered out the front for a post-mortem on our respective nights. The consensus of the group was that we should probably just never speak of this hotel ever again and move on our merry way as soon as was humanly possible.

This day held a lot of "little bit up, little bit down" that was combined with the huffing, puffing and groaning of some sick people. Once again, the boys pointed out blue sheep on the far side of the valley along with some wild deer. Both near and far herds of yak and zhong, a cross-breed between a yak and a water buffalo, could be seen. The ground became tricky with large patches of scree to cross.

Eventually we descended to a flat bridge over the Kone Khola. Immediately on the other side we commenced a series of steep switchbacks with eventually broke into a flat patch of ground where an enterprising herder had set up a shop for all the exhausted trekkers. We ended up stopping for a rather delightful lemon tea. Our New Zealand sometimes trail companions took the opportunity to refresh their fluid levels. I noted that I had a slight headache. Erring on the side of caution, I raised this with Dorje and Mike on the off chance that this was a more serious indicator of altitude sickness. With some relevant questioning, they were confident to announce that the headache was not as serious as I had worried and I should be okay to continue after having consumed a couple of paracetamol. Leaving after the others, Dorje and I brought up the tail of the group. He recommended that we walk slowly to our next stop.

Image: Kim Stanley-Eyles

The views were spectacular but it was hard to take it all in when you're concentrating on just putting one foot in front of another. Finally we drifted in to Thorung Phedi (4,450 metres) for lunch at around 10:30. Behind the protective glass of the Hotel New Phedi, we absorbed some of the brilliant sun until it became too warm to sit there. Despite the relative remoteness of the area, the hotels here boasted hot showers, heated dining rooms and even satellite telephone services.

In keeping with our history of helping others, Dorje asked if Kim, Mike and I could have a look at one of the Israeli girls who was in a spot of bother. We found her out on the stone paved forecourt of the hotel. Sitting in the warm sun, she had pulled her socks off to reveal a magnificent set of blisters on both feet and heels.

With her broken English and Kim's broken Spanish, we were able to figure out the problems. Having patched up her feet we advised her to move slowly and to rest them as much as possible. At this point, telling her not to finish the climb to the pass would have been pointless. Besides, whichever way you looked at it, she would be looking at a long walk either up or down. Little did we know how hard the last stretch of today's walk would end up being.

Chapter 7 - Over the top, chaps

"The traveler sees what he sees, the tourist sees what he has come to see." – G. K. Chesterton

Our day was to end at Base Camp (High Camp) some 475 metres above us at Thorung Pedi. Not surprisingly this would take us around two hours of seemingly near vertical switchbacks. The sun, where we ate lunch, or attempted to, was actually hot under the glass windows and ceiling of the restaurant. But we knew that to be a false impression of the temperature outside in the wind, especially with the sun quickly heading for the sides of the valley. This would mean that the temperature on the trails would drop dramatically. Stark bare mountainsides in hues and shades of grey surrounded us in an other-worldly landscape. The contrast in the bright, clear sunshine gave everything a sharpness and definition over distance. Even at this altitude, the occasional bird would drift into view or spiral on the thermals rising from the warmed rocks.

Knowing that our day's end was in sight, figuratively not literally, we shouldered our bags and began the climb. Here our walking poles came into their own; seeking their grip amongst the loose shale beneath our feet. Soon, we were strung out along the trail with Mike and Sandra somewhere towards the front. Their almost boundless energy, while flagging, still kept them well in the lead.

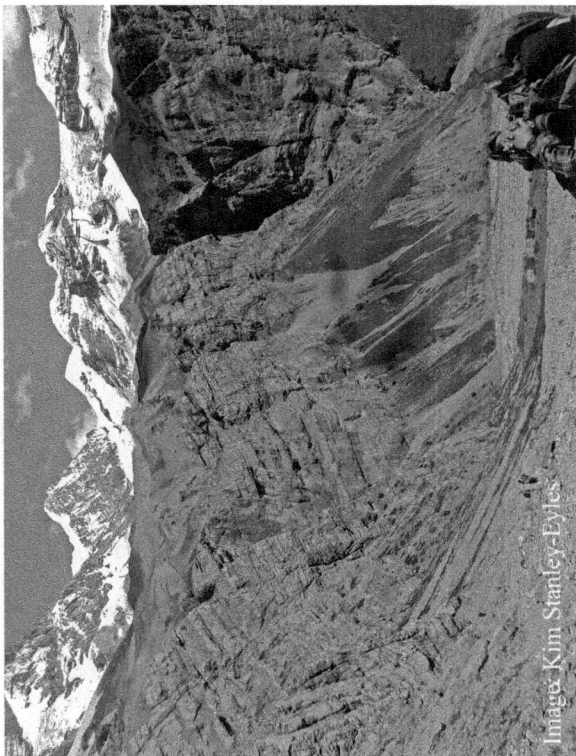

Image: Kim Stanley-Eyles

Kim, Margaret and I slowly trudged up the incline. We took to stopping each time the trail cut back on itself for a breather and to take in the view. While the climb was easy for the boys, they took turns keeping an eye on us. I don't remember who was there regularly. Trekking in tough conditions wraps you in your own little world. Often your eyes are on the ground; one foot in front of the other. "Bisari bisari," say the boys, "slowly slowly." We each had our own technique for continuing. Kim would spy a rock large enough to sit on up ahead and make that her goal; the reward would be sitting and resting on it for a few minutes. By now, Kim had also started to develop the trail cough and was finding the going difficult.

Base Camp is very close to Thorung Pedi; around two kilometres. But those two kilometres took the three of us around 80 minutes to complete. The shadows were already lengthening. Mike and Sandra were already ensconced in their rooms. We had a "boys" room and a "girls" room here. Base Camp nestles in a relatively flat patch of ground between several shale covered hills. Several trails lead off in different directions from this location although its main purpose is as the staging point for the run up to the pass. Generally speaking people are normally coming from the east. The usual method of following the Annapurna circuit is in an anti-clockwise direction. From time to time, the seriously intrepid traveller may come west down from the pass but normally a local person may make the trip instead. Base Camp is an interesting place. I was told it is the site of a 200 bed hotel with solar lights and satellite television but apparently has no hot water.

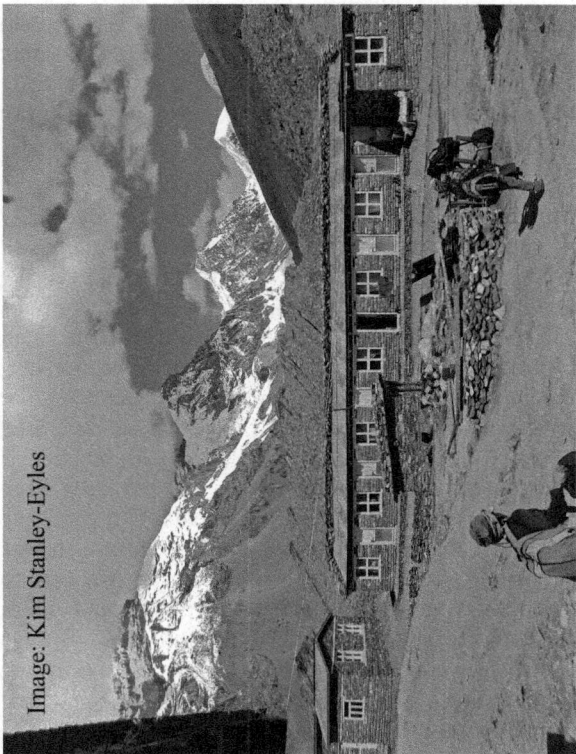

Image: Kim Stanley-Eyles

There is virtually no vegetation, just some hardy lichens and mosses, and yet where the waste water runs from the kitchens, some hardy short grasses appear to survive. A few birds have learnt to scavenge food scraps or hunt the local rodents that scratch out a living hiding amongst the rocks. During the middle of winter, no one is here and the entire place may become buried in snow.

Having found our rooms, I sauntered over to the restaurant to see what everyone else was doing. Many of the faces from the trail were here; the English boys, the Spanish brothers, the Israelis and even the lovely ladies from New Zealand. Many of the groups sat and chatted with other trekkers. The large main room was crowded. But in a sight I gather is not very common in other trekking groups, but was a regular activity with ours, Kim and I were joined by Dorje, Dhan, Kanchha, La Har and Purna This practice is considered unusual since porters will normally keep themselves separate from their clients. Out came the cards and the laughter began again in earnest. It was actions like these that had other porters wanting to know how to work with Australians and other trekkers wanting to know if they could hire our guys when we were finished with them. Dorje was trying to exchange information with people as potential future clients.

What was very funny to us was that the game of 'Spit' actually bet us up the mountain. Our porters had taught it to other card-playing porters during social time on the trip. In the smaller communal room more commonly used by the porters away from the trekkers, we could hear the tell-tailed laughter and hands thumping on tables as the race to sort all your cards and claim the smallest pile played out again and again.

Lost in my thoughts and thoroughly tired, I occasionally chatted with some of the other trekkers or tried to get some video from the relatively warm comfort of the dining room. High above us, Mike had decided to "climb high, sleep low" and was photographing the camp from a lookout several hundred metres away. Kim was wondering how it was possible he still had energy to walk further up. A few hardy souls appeared to have joined him and it would be they who most likely had the best sleep that night. Around us the high peaks sparkled brightly as the sun began its relentless descent over the horizon and the light slowly closed in. Some high level clouds began to form around some of the mountain tops.

At 15:45 Mike came in and asked for Kim and I to urgently come outside for a suspected severe case of altitude sickness. It turned out to be our Israeli friend from lunchtime with the blistered feet. She had reached Base Camp only to collapse. She was presenting some fairly significant signs to suggest the onset of High Altitude Pulmonary Edema (HAPE).

The risk of Acute Mountain Sickness (AMS) can begin once a traveller ascends above 2,500 metres. If a climber or trekker continues to ascend at speed and without acclimatisation, this condition will become fatal through either HAPE or High Altitude Cerebral Edema (HACE). Often the sufferer will not

147

acknowledge the signs and symptoms, blaming them on a range of trip preparation inadequacies or other minor medical conditions. There is no currently way to predict who may be afflicted. Previous journeys where a traveller has not been affect are no guarantee of immunity. Best practice in treatment is to immediately descend.

The woman's breathing was laboured with a cough. She was having extreme difficulty with the effort of walking up hill and had both a rapid heart and respiration rates that was lasting well after the end of the exercise. Our patient was disoriented, had appeared wearing only one shoe without realising she had even lost it, and refused to recognise the serious possibilities of continuing. According to her travelling companion, this had happened before when in Tibet: they had been forced to descend rapidly thereby preventing the completion of the walk they had been taking at that stage. She point blank refused to accept the need to descend right now. As far as she was concerned, nothing would prevent her from cresting the pass.

This was a condition which we had no real experience or understanding of, just a basic knowledge to recognise the potential seriousness of the situation. We decided to locate and call on the services of a young doctor from Sydney who was trekking with his new wife on their honeymoon. Our paths had coincided back as far as Manang.

He quickly arrived and conducted an assessment of the girl. It was his considered opinion that she should descend immediately and spend the night at Thorung

Pedi before considering trying for the pass tomorrow. Ideally he wanted her to not attempt it at all but she at least agreed to head down for the night. Night was closing in as the sun rapidly slid behind the mountains. Several porters from different trekking groups volunteered to take her down the steep trail in the fading light. Taking it in turns, they hoisted her onto their backs and began a rapid descent, her companion in tow with one porter helping to carry the bags. Within 40 minutes, the porters were back with the news that she was safely ensconced at the hotels below. We couldn't believe that they had gone down and back again in such a quick time; the Nepali porters really are truly a hardy people.

Returning to the dining room, we settled in to chat with the doctor and his good wife before someone else called for his attention to check out apparent grit in their eye. Kim managed to slip away and was found with the majority of porters in a back room watching pirated Bollywood films It was an early night as our start the next morning would be long before the sun considered coming up.

Like most of the other groups, our members weren't up to eating much. Sandra had Swiss potato rosti with cheese for tea. The English boys were faring better than most but were short of funds. They opted for the local daal bhaat, which our porters always ate. The deal with this meal was that you could have unlimited "top ups" as you finished each part of the meal. In this way they could eat as much as they liked; and they certainly did.

Rösti is originally a Swiss dish primarily made with fried grated or chucks of potato and egg. Sometimes Nepali menus refer to them as "hashed browns" but they bear no resemblance to those served as a certain commercial restaurant. In fact I prefer the Nepali version at any time.

It was a very very cold night. Margaret .joked that you'd have to be desperate for the toilet during the night to get out of your sleeping bag, don your boots, grab your headlamp and venture some distance away to a dark, cold smelly squat toilet.

Day 12 was Friday September 18th and would be a long and arduous one. My sleep during the night, while quite good for me, had been interrupted. Not so much from the cold since my down sleeping bag was quite excellent but more for the sound of a rat rummaging through the side pockets of my bag to devour the remains of a chapatti that someone had left there from the day before. At this altitude even turning over in the sleeping bag leaves you heaving with the lack of oxygen. It takes a while for normal breathing to return. Our alarms were set for 04:00 when we began packing our things away. By 04:30 we were ready for breakfast but once again I could not face food. The others had long since given up being concerned about my lack of interest in eating. It was a side effect of the altitude for me.

At 05:00 we set off on the climb to the pass. We had been warned to make sure our head torches were of a good quality with fresh batteries. Now we began to see why. The false dawn was barely on the horizon. Air temperature was below freezing and the rocky ground was rough if very well-trodden. One foot in front of the other with a large contingent of other trekkers and their support staff, we began climbing the path. The line of bobbing head torches looked quite surreal in the crisp, cold air. Following the heels of the person in front as they flashed into your head lamp, I didn't see in the dark the treacherous drop off to our right. Only using the modern convenience of Google Earth can one truly appreciate the type of terrain we traversed.

We only had to cover approximately two kilometres as the crow flies and climb about 491 metres but the oxygen content at this altitude is 60% of that available at sea level. Every step became an effort. The terrain slowly began to emerge as the sun rose closer to dawn. All around was a desolate landscape of rock, shale, scree and mountains. As the light increased, so did the contrast and the landscape began to take on three dimensions with the clarity of pure air. The alpine plants and flowers began to take shape. Fortunately we were rising across the slope rather than directly up, otherwise this might have taken me all day. Again I entered that personal state of being which meant I was the only person to exist; one foot in front of the other. Don't stop. "Slowly slowly. Bisari bisari." My mind began to drift and thoughts washed over me from different directions. The thoughts became my worst enemy as they wore at my determination to keep moving. At my core a small thought kept striking back. I was about to go higher than any member of my family had ever gone before. It was only a little further. The sun needed to be get a little higher then I could enjoy the view.

After that, it would be a lovely downhill stroll to Muktinath.

At one point the path became flat, compared to the surrounding landscape, and we were travelling down into a gully where we crossed a flat metal bridge. Then we began climbing again. As we crested the ridge, we doubled back on the other side. Now the climbing began again. Every breath was an effort and getting my feet to work properly was hard work. Eventually we broke out onto comparatively flat ground only to discover, in the middle of nowhere, a tea house serving the trekkers as they passed through. We took tea and were surprised to see a mob of about 30 goats standing around picking through the sparse vegetation of mosses and lichens. Focusing on the promised hot tea, it occurred to me that it was 07:00 and we had already been on the path for two hours.

As we prepared to move on, there was an anguished cry from a Nepali man. It turned out that he was the one who owned the goats. In the time we had been sitting there, they had all turned tail and disappeared. He had searched in the vicinity and they could not be found. They could be anywhere on the mountain in any direction by now. Their value was the equivalent of about two year's wages. With the Hindu festival of Dashain less than a week away, he was about to make a lot of money selling the goats for sacrifice. Now all of that was gone. We left him to his uncharacteristically public display of distress and carried on climbing. There was nothing we could do for him, and we had barely the energy to walk.

The angle of ascent became steeper as the day grew brighter. The orderly mass of guides, porters and trekkers had become a ragged line spread out along the ridges and through gullies. Just as you thought you might be reaching your destination, you would turn the corner and be confronted with more open ground and the trail, always the trail. There were several mental breakdowns along the way including me although I didn't end up a gibbering mess. All the while, Kim kept coaching me. Talking in my ear and pushing me on. We played the game to spot the sitting rocks ahead, and shared them when we eventually reached them.

Up ahead, the word went out that the mob of goats had been spotted. They had made a bolt for the pass and had discovered some particularly nice lichen to munch on. The news went back down the trail and we hoped it wouldn't be too long before the owner caught up to them. Somewhere on a mountain to our left, possibly an unnamed one in front of Purkung (6,126 metres), Sandra spotted a small avalanche and Kim quickly set up her camera to try and catch some of the action.

Then from behind came the sound of a donkey bell. Coming past was the Israeli girl from last night. She had hired the pony to get her to the pass as quickly as possible. This urged me on and eventually I was the last of our group to arrive at the pass just before 09:00. I joined somewhere close to 60 people as they gathered near a tea house at the crest of the pass. Yes, a tea house on top of the pass! Inside a soldier was stamping the trekking permits. We shared our meagre supply of Mars Bars and Snickers with the boys over cups of steaming hot lemon drinks purchased from the small building. La Har was laughing. Even shy Purna had a smile on his face. Many tears were shed amongst the various strangers. Photos were taken of us in front of the official sign which was almost buried in the remnants of prayer flags and handmade signs to stake the claim of previous successful visitors.

We had made it to the Thorung La Pass (5,416 metres) considered to be the world's highest, and possibly oldest, continually open pass although in the depths of winter, the snow can be over three metres deep. It was nestled between the peaks of Yakwakang (6,482 metres) and Khatungkang (6,484 metres). From here we could look east over the mountains that had been our constant companions for the better part of nearly a fortnight. To the west we looked out over the Kali Gandaki valley to the peaks bordering the ancient kingdom of Mustang. The ground gently sloped away from us until it seemed to just end in nothingness. The sky was a vibrant blue. The nearby peaks were sharply outlined with their white mantels. Nearby ground was a mix of oranges, umbers, browns, greys and slates. We each let our minds absorb the majesty of our surroundings. Off to the north, Kim had walked to spend some time alone with her thoughts, to remember her late mother and ring a prayer bell purchased in her honour.

Image: Mike Evans

The air blew coldly around us reminding us exactly what the wind-chill could do to us if we stayed too long. That was on top of what we could expect when the winds got up from the Kali Gandaki Nadi. The winds down in the valley could reach speeds of over 70 kilometres per hour. Up here they would be faster as the narrow valleys compressed and directed the air flow.

Having spent such a short time at the pass, it soon became time for us to begin the descent. With a small amount of surprise, I noted that many of the other travellers had already departed. A few hardy souls remained presumably in an effort to get some unobstructed photos of the surrounding area. A shudder of relief passed through me at the thought of going downhill rather than the hard slog to climb up. Perhaps I was being naive or maybe it was the exhaustion and lack of oxygen but I had not considered what a pain walking down hill could be. The trail seemed benign enough to start off. A gently sloping path clearly picked its way through the scree and tumbled boulders. Our steps lively and packs feeling like they weighed half, we bounced our way down towards our ultimate destination at Muktinath.

Again we strung out in a long line, this time Kim and Kanchha leading the way.

It was time to enjoy a more relaxing walk down from the pass. But the ground gradually became steeper. Our thighs began to feel the familiar burn of continually walking downhill. The shale became more coarse and loose. In the distance the peaks of the Upper Mustang danced in and out of drifting clouds. The sun reflected brightly off the surrounding valley. Every so often we would step across discarded thick steel cables about the diameter of my wrist. At one point, Kanchha asked Kim with a cheeky grin on his face if she trusted him. "Of course I do," she said. With one of his patented double click sounds, he grabbed her hand and began running head long down the ever increasing slope. For every step, they would slide two or more metres before plunging into the next step giggling with glee like a couple of children. Out of breath they eventually stopped and waited for the rest of us to catch up; huge grins plastered across their faces.

A series of giant terraces appeared about half way down the decline alongside the dry bed of the Thorong Khola. Reaching the first one, we discovered our trail companions scattered across it laying on the grass in the glorious sunshine. Sandra and Dhan had gotten there a good half hour before anyone else. From below a team of Nepali workers could be heard being urged on by the man in front. Around 30 in the team, they carried with them another of the thick steel cables, estimated to be around a tonne in weight. They were arranged so that the cable was folded back in the middle like a point and the workers were strung out every few metres along its length with the leader in the central point calling the simultaneous steps. Dhan explained that they were being carried up and down the other side of the pass to build a bridge. This back breaking work was at least a source of income for these people but it had to be done one step at a time.

Image: Kim Stanley-Eyles

I watch again in the video the one step forward, half a step back; the call of the leader urging them on.

Having rested there for around 15-20 minutes, we hoisted bags again and carried on down the slope. The sun was high in the sky and the time well past midday before we stopped for lunch at a collection of buildings around Champerbu tea house. At this altitude the temperature was surprisingly hot and we took shelter from the blowing dust inside. Exhaustion took over and we crashed out on the Tibetan rugs scattered on wooden benches to catch a little nap while waiting for the food to arrive.

Sandra and Dan had finished their meals and left early to walk to Muktinath. Sandra was keen to make sure that the rooms we were to stay at were still available. Feeling refreshed, the rest of the group gathered themselves for the last push down the mountain. We passed smaller terraces and the occasional yak herders' shelters. With the sun descending towards the distant peaks we eventually reached the white boundary wall of the temple at Muktinath-Chumig Gyatsa. This temple site is revered by both Buddhists and Hindus alike and is said to be the source of the Gandaki River rising from the 108 springs within the temple grounds. Many make annual pilgrimages from faraway places, originally on foot, but now often as passengers in 4WD vehicles. We found it was quite normal for different faiths to share sites of worship in this way, and it was a very amicable and respectful relationship. Within the Jwala Mai temple burn two holy flames that are fed by natural gas straight from the ground. One bubbles up through the water.

At around 15:00, we eventually arrived in the town of Muktinath (3,760 metres) after having been on the trail for ten hours. The ascent had been 419 metres before descending 1,656 metres covering 14 kilometres of hard slog. After 11 days we again heard the strident sounds of vehicles. I know a few of us felt a little saddened by the return to wide roads, exhaust fumes and the ever present variety of horns. The sound of feet on gravel and heavy breathing at the start of the day was replaced by the thrum of civilisation. Walking just a little further we arrived in Ranipauwa which is considered to be so close that it is often counted as one and the same place. Somewhere nearby the strains of Bob Marley drifted towards us as we crossed the last low bridge of the first stream in days. Stall holders called to us with their wares but we didn't have the energy. Staggering along the street we found the source of the music coming from the Hotel Bob Marley. Our destination lay right next door at the Hotel Mona Lisa where warm showers waited. Kim and I were done in while Margaret and Sandra went shopping.

Kanchha took Sandra to the monastery to see the holy men and the pilgrims bathing in the pools and running under the 108 water spouts.

Settled in, but needing to wind down, we couldn't resist stretching some of the aches on the balcony while checking out the local vendors. In the street opposite our hotel, stalls were set up displaying a range of wares including stones from the nearby river. A smiling woman, who ran the stall, eagerly chatted with tourists and pilgrims alike. A permanently installed vertical frame was covered in dozens of locally woven scarves, hats and mittens. On a low, portable, fold-out display sat singing bowls, jewellery, bangles, carvings and rounded local river stones. When split through these stone revealed fossils buried in their centre; evidence of creatures that had once lived in the sea millions of years previously but who had ended up here some 3,760 metres above sea level. Several khukuri or traditional knives, more styled for tourists than for real work, sat at the back of the display. We joked and laughed our way through the haggling. We played the game and her grin nearly split her face. The cut and thrust of shopping left us with some small but significant souvenirs to take home. As we later found, this wasn't her only business. She ran a series of stalls and the internet cafe across from our hotel.

The boys took their leave and were off to enjoy the evening after the hard climb. I tried the satellite internet but it failed to connect. Kim wanted to eat yak for her meal and it was on the menu. Dorje, however, didn't believe that it would be fresh enough. He recommended waiting until we got to Jomsom. After a desperately needed meal, I headed for bed and I didn't even hear the Jewish New Year's party going on next door until the wee hours.

My legs were shaking like jelly and my thighs were burning from the effort but nothing could taint the success of having crested the highest pass in the world. It was an exhilarating day.

Chapter 8 - Bound for separation

"To awaken quite alone in a strange town is one of the pleasantest sensations in the world." – Freya Starkl

September 19th already and I awoke with the realisation that this would be Kim's last full day but at least it would be all downhill walking. She had to return to work earlier than the rest of us.

Everyone reported that they were feeling sore. My thighs and hips were attempting to give me a full report of the previous day's efforts and the attendant damage. Our morning was bright with a clear sky overhead. Standing on the first floor balcony, I looked down to spot a grinning La Har with an ever present cup of tea in his hand. His cheery good morning made the aches and pains from the previous day seem unimportant. Around him streamed a long line of pilgrims heading up to Muktinath-Chumig Gyatsa. Weighed down with everything including their own food, they made their way patiently to the temple to wait in the growing admission lines to bath in the two pools and run under the 108 sacred springs.

Our trader from the previous night had her stalls stretched down the street once again. The passing pilgrims made use of a line of prayer wheels. A young man roared past on his motorbike; quiet by modern standards but sounding like a jet engine after 11 days of our remote quiet. To my right, a woman milked a water buffalo for the daily supply. In the brightly contrasted morning light, the surrounding white peaks sparkled against the pale blue sky.

This side of the pass is more like a desert with patches of greenery only around settlements, along the banks of the river and, further down, where irrigation was in use. However where trees grew, they were often of a reasonable size and lush. Some of the lower slopes around the river showed evidence of erosion. The ground outside of the town was dry and dusty. Each step raised a brown puff that sought entry to every gap in our clothing.

The other side of the valley is sparsely populated. Settlements are marked by the assorted patches of green, olive, yellow and pink scattered along the valley floor. Our morning's trail meandered alongside low cracked dry mud walls topped with a light thatch of straw.

Despite the pain, I felt light on my feet. Travelling downhill we could get a good pace which was often interrupted as we had time to take in the view again. There were numerous stops for photographs particularly north across the terraces over the valley into Upper Mustang. We passed many stone buildings under construction. The group began to string out down the path before gathering on the outskirts of Jharkot (3,550 metres). Amongst the ancient remains of a former palace of the King of Mustang stood the red rendered walls of the Sakya Gompa and Traditional Medicine Centre. For the tiny fee of NPR100 and after carefully removing our boots, we were granted access to the monastery. We were able to gaze upon ancient art stained by the centuries of soot from countless butter candles, some of it estimated to be 800 years old. Towards the front of the small room, the artwork had been carefully restored. The characters had been cleaned back and seemed as vibrant as the day they had been painted. Around the walls were pictures of various members of the monastery. The high ceiling windows lit the room with a golden light especially when it landed on the large statue of Buddha and the golden tapestries above. A modern touch was evident in the little twinkling electric lights carefully arranged along the wall behind the ancient Buddha.

Up a narrow staircase outside the prayer room we eventually came out onto the roof. From here we could gaze across the valley and into the grounds of the property. Below us students moved from class to class in the small school. Across the roof tops, modern solar devices could be seen; either power or water. Overhead a small helicopter, the first of several tourist flights for the morning, swooped in to land on one of the two helipads at Muktinath. To the west, we could see down to the end of the valley near Kagbeni. To the north-east, over the rising mountains some 40 kilometres away lay the border with Tibet. Overhead a few lonely raptors slowly spiralled on the gently forming thermals.

Descending to the courtyard, we reacquired our boots in front of the paintings of the karmic wheel of life. These appeared to have been painted on a cloth attached to the wall of the veranda. Gathering our day-bags, we re-joined the boys to explore buildings surrounding the monastery. The outer walls were mud rendered, some of them whitewashed, and showed little sign of water damage suggesting the tiny amount of precipitation the region receives. Various little alleyways led to our left and right, either up or down between the buildings. A descending curving path came in from our left around one building. Across its top was a square archway guarded on either side by obviously male (Pho-lha) and female (Phuk-lha) statues from the Bon religion. Bon is said to pre-date Buddhism although according to Wikipedia's entry on the Bon, records only go back around the 9th or 10th centuries after religious suppression by Tibetan Buddhism. According to the boys it is still practised to a small extent and in this region we would see a few examples as we travelled about. This region has seen centuries of refugee migrations from the north. Evidence of this could clearly be seen on the far side of the valley. Mike pointed out a range of small dark specks which were caves. It was in these caves that the Tibetans would live. Over the centuries erosion had changed the level of the valley floor meaning that many of the caves can now only be reached by repelling from above or climbing up treacherously steep shale banks. Often they can be seen several hundred metres above the river. Access is restricted because they are in Upper Mustang which requires a separate trekking permit.

In the delightfully hot sun, we continued on our path until we reached the village of Khingar (3,280 metres) where Kim engaged in another enjoyable haggling session with a local woman sitting at her loom, for one of her vibrant scarves. With broad grins on both sides, Kim secured a beautiful purple one at a reasonable price as a gift for a friend back home. It was lovely and soft with the colours coming from home dying techniques. A short while later we passed another woman who was also weaving scarves. Her prices were much higher and we declined to stop. It was time for a tea break and we selected the courtyard of a small tea house charmingly called Romeo and Juliet Lodge & Restaurant. The walls were bricks painted a chocolate colour and the corner posts were a bright yellow. The edge of the roof was trimmed in stones to prevent it lifting in strong winds. Resting under the shade of some brightly coloured umbrellas in the quickly heating sun, we took our refreshments. It was there that we encountered two women from Mustang, a mother and daughter I believe, in their best traditional Tibetan clothes who were heading for Muktinath, a trip of 7 days by foot. Mike with his usual affable smile and the assistance of the boys engaged these shy women in conversation. Kim, Margaret and Sandra immediately became enthralled with their clothes. Dressed in a similar nature, the main part of their garb was a sleeveless black dress or vest and black skirt. The sleeves themselves were of brightly coloured and patterned material; one in bronze, the other in green. Around their waists were a sort of cummerbund in blues, purples and burgundies. Over the top, they wore a short skirt or apron in a variety of colours. Around their necks, they wore prayer beads. They kindly posed for pictures with Kim, Margaret and Sandra before we hit the trail again.

In the distance, four wheel drive vehicles could be heard travelling from Jomsom to Kagbeni transporting pilgrims. The breeze was beginning to pick up by mid-morning. We reached a fork in the road and a decision needed to be made. Should we take the path to the left leading to Ekle Bhatti or the lower right path to Kagbeni? Mike had been in this area before and was anxious to show us the delights of Kagbeni, one of the gateways into Upper Mustang. Margaret and I were beginning to feel the rigours of our journey and really wanted to head direct to Jomsom. Dorje needed a break too. Despite his stoic nature, it was quickly becoming obvious that something was not right. He was taking more breaks than had been normal for him. He wouldn't say anything, I believed, because this was the first trek that he had put together himself and he did not want anything to go wrong. Mike also picked up on his extra breaks. A check of my backpack that he carried showed that the vertical alloy reinforcing bars were bent and had been pushing into his back. Mike managed to push them almost back into place, but it would still be uncomfortable carrying. Without Dorje's knowledge, we discussed our options for getting him to take a break. The plan was to find a jeep which Margaret and I would use because we weren't feeling well.

The difficulty was in locating a jeep that was going our way and not already loaded to the gunnels with passengers. As the large Hindu festival of Dashain was approaching, dozens of pilgrims were making their way to Muktinath. Very few vehicles were making their way back to Jomsom at this time of day.

Since Mike was eager to show us Kagbeni, we veered to the right and began making our way towards the small settlement down by the river.

The boys had stayed at the tea house for a meal while we walked on with Dorje.

The remaining porters and all our backpacks veered left to the south; planning on meeting us in Jomsom. On the western side of the intersecting Kali Gandaki river valley in front of us, a zigzagging trail climbed the steeply inclined mountain heading into Mustang. We crossed a flat plain following our narrow path and came across a series of stacked stones left by various travellers. With due care not to take stones from anyone else's pile, we built our own to mark the passing by of the Thorung Five. Our vantage point allowed us to look down on the town of Kagbeni. Below us came the sound of large machinery although it was unclear if it was agricultural in nature or some sort of road building work in progress. Through a series of switchbacks, we made our way down cutting over the roads and past bright pink paddocks full of buckwheat waving in the breeze.

Making our way between buildings, we entered the narrow walkway running north-south through the ancient town of Kagbeni (2,800 metres). The town sits on the banks of the broad Kali Gandaki (river) and is one of the gateways into Upper Mustang. From here trekkers can use their $US500 access permit which will allow them 10 days in this ancient hilltop kingdom.

Mike led the way taking us directly to the lodge where he had stayed previously. It was a lovely two-storey, well-constructed building with a large dining room called the New Asia Trekkers House. Seating was traditional benches covered with woven thin mats. Dorje fell asleep on the grass in the glorious sun. After the last couple of days up so high, the sun had begun to feel almost too hot but he was happy. Margaret and I fell asleep in the dining room on the surprisingly comfortable bench seats.

Kim, Mike and Sandra took to wandering the streets. Their explorations located a sign imitating a certain international food chain but representing a local hotel and restaurant. The high walls of the buildings were of stone construction and would provide adequate protection from the strong Mustang winds, which had already started to pick up. Several of the small, tough horses local to this area were wearing traditional hand-woven saddle rugs, and they came across an un-manned water-powered mill grinding flour. In various streams, locals worked in the water washing clothes. Across the flat, broad river bed, large clouds of dust travelled north at surprising speed.

Above the pastel colours of the western shore of the Kali Gandaki, hermit caves looked out across the valley. Still in use today, some monks may take up residence for 25 or more years. They will follow strict regimes of meditation attempting to gain enlightenment. People will check on them from time to time although their needs are often very simple. Food and drink is often minimal and it has been known for hermits to actually die in their pursuits.

Having quickly downed some lunch, we set out on foot along the river towards Jomsom. As we left the boundaries of the town, we could understand the warnings we had been given. Bandanas quickly moved into place; Kim and I tying our hats to our heads at the same time. The Mustang winds began to be driven north up the valley from about 11:00 each morning. All flights into and out of the valley usually stop at this time, since the swirling nature of the winds makes flying treacherous. Mike pulled out his portable weather station and recorded head wind speeds over 75 kilometres per hour.

Walking became a supreme effort. It was head down and foot in front of foot walking on flat, overlapping river stones. Every placement ran the risk of being unstable. Each break was taken behind large boulders when it would be safe enough to lift the bandana and try to sip some water. Huge plumes of dust roared up the valley, scrubbing their way around rocks, gaining entrance to every gap in our clothing. I began to think perhaps the decision to visit Kagbeni had not been the wisest but in reality, the issue was actually about when we departed. We should have left perhaps an hour earlier and even that was purely my opinion. It might have been nice perhaps to stay overnight and set out for Jomsom first thing in the morning.

Image: Mike Evans

From our trail we had no hope of coming across any vehicles. It was not until we reached Ekle Bhatti that we could take a decent break out of the wind. As we staggered into the village, we were met by Dhan, Kanchha, La Har and Purna sitting in a local shop. Gratefully I sank into the plastic chair and sipped on a cold Coke.

The glass bottles the soft drinks came in had been a source of amusement and amazement to us all on the journey. Empty bottles were carefully collected and taken down the mountains for cleaning and refilling, before being brought back up to the tea houses. Many of them are opaque with age and use, and sporting dates as far back as the early 1970's. When the roads stop, these bottles are carried back up the mountains for days by donkey or pony train, or even by porter.

The wind blasted its way past the village. Through the grubby windows of the shop we could see the extensive range of small items for sale to passing pilgrims and tourists. I don't think it would have been possible to keep the windows clean out there, irrespective of the effort put in. Quite possibly, the glass wasn't dirty at all. More likely it had been sand blasted by years of dust storms. Sweeping would have seemed like a pointless task and yet a woman was doing just that.

As we rested, over the sound of the wind could be heard local music playing loudly and badly distorted as though someone had poured sand onto the speakers. A jeep swung out of the dust and squealed to a halt in front of the store. As the driver turned off the engine, the music stopped.

Dorje descended on the driver to see if there was any space for passengers. After some in-depth negotiations, our bags began to be loaded on the roof. As is the usual practice, no strapping was used to hold them down. With the bags in place, all the boys except for La Har climbed aboard followed by Margaret and I. La Har remained behind to guide the others down the trail. We waved goodbye to Kim, Mike and Sandra as the jeep began to bounce over the rounded stones. La Har and Kim laughingly waved goodbye to the precariously balanced baggage on the roof, wondering if it would still be there at the jeeps destination. The driver turned the music back on at full volume. While the music was fine culturally, the volume just pounded through our heads. The driver must have sensed the problem it was causing and he turned it down much to our relief.

The road wandered along the side of the valley and rose above the river. We weren't too high up but high enough that if the driver had bounced the wrong way, we most likely would have been killed before the vehicle stopped rolling over. It was narrow enough that passing on coming vehicles proved to be entertaining at the least. And yes, I am talking in the usual Australian form of understatement. To our left perhaps a dozen or more individual dust storms flowed up the wide valley, some of them five and six storeys tall. We bounced around inside the cabin of the jeep; heads coming dangerously close to hitting the roof. The boys were grinning from ear to ear and laughing at our expressions.

After 20 minutes of being thrown around like washing in a tumble dryer, we arrived on the outskirts of Jomsom (2,720 metres). The boys hoisted the backpacks (yes, amazingly they were still all there)and led us through the narrow meandering streets of the town until we reached the Hotel Alka Mar-Copolo (read Marco Polo). Passing through the first door of this whitewashed building into the foyer, we were surprised to be taken through the back door, across a dirt laneway and into another building. This was the dining room of the hotel. Passing along a narrow corridor into a courtyard garden with a heavily laden apple tree, we were shown the hotel rooms. Struggling up a flight of stairs, I followed the boys as they stowed our bags in adjoining rooms. A check of the room found comfortable beds, ample power points and a generous bath room with huge shower and a sit-down flushing toilet! After taking a nice hot shower to wash away the dirt, I was then able to sit out the front on the balcony to update my diary and enjoy the snow-capped views to the south east of Nilgiri (North) (7,061 metres) in the Nilgiri Himal and east to the Muktinath Himal and Timchibhuk (4,993) while in the background sat Khatungkang (6,484 metres) and Thorung Peak.

Below me sat the main part of the town. Between us and the river was the airport. The town spread north and south, mostly comprising low, flat-roofed buildings of stone. On the slopes above the east bank of the river sat the village of Thinigaon.

Approximately an hour and a half after separating, the remaining group finally made it to the hotel. They were exhausted and covered from head to foot in dust. Kim, Mike and Sandra retreated to their respective rooms for a blissful, well-earned hot shower. Kim's legs were shaking with the effort.

Sandra, Mike and Kim told me it was one of the hardest days walking they had ever had. The rough stones slipped underfoot jarring the legs, and having to lean into the 70km/hr wind was exhausting as you still had to brace for when the wind suddenly slackened and started again. Every centimetre of skin had to be covered to prevent sand blasting, and they could only stop and take a drink behind the very few large boulders in the wide river plain that could cut the wind. Sandra's toes were tender for days requiring a foam support sleeve. Kim's calves spasmed painfully for the rest of her time in Nepal

Dinner was somewhat sombre since it was Kim's last night. Sadly she missed out on yak again as it was not fresh. Instead we feasted on roast chicken with chips and vegetables, followed by chocolate pudding and apple lassi.

Lassi is a yoghurt drink, often with fruit mixed through. It is a refreshing beverage on a hot day. We highly recommend searching up the dozens, if not hundreds, of recipes on the internet. I have even had it served as a replacement for custard in a dessert.

The boys all took time to be with Kim as she had become a real favourite. Even just watching local television was enough.

Staggering back to the room, we rearranged the bags for her flight in the morning. Having descended

1,080 metres over 19 kilometres that day, we managed a reasonably good night's sleep. The next day would be a new phase. Not an anticlimax as such, just a new trip, almost separate from the previous 12 days.

Chapter 9 - Where are the hot springs?

"Our happiest moments as tourists always seem to come when we stumble upon one thing while in pursuit of something else." — Lawrence Block

It was a sad morning as Kim and La Har were leaving the group. Work commitments meant that Kim had to return to Australia. Since La Har had been her porter, he too was finished with the trip at this stage. But as a final sign to the boys that she was not above a bit of friendly rivalry, she carried her own fully laden backpack down from the room and into their midst. As I watch the video again, I can see young Purna with a grave look of concern as she approached. He had obviously not been party to the constant joking between Kim and Kanchha about who was the strongest and was obviously worried that a tourist would be carrying their own pack anywhere.

As the others arrived, the general morning's sorting of the backpacks occurred. The boys chatted amongst themselves as they strapped their personal gear to our bags. I noticed a large cardboard box arrive which was being fussed over by the boys. A ball of string was produced and amongst a lot of chatter, the box was carefully bound in a manner of which my grandmother would have been proud. Twice around each side and then a multi-strand rope handle woven into the lot. Much to my surprise, it contained apples, grown just down the valley in Marpha. They were a present for Dhan's wife and Kim had been asked to arrange delivery on her return to Kathmandu. A cousin of Dorje's, Ram, had been organised to be Kim's guide for the couple of days she would be in the capital before returning to Australia.

Around 06:30, after teary farewells and a gift from Kim to the boys of Australian playing cards, Kim and the box of apples left with several of the boys for the airport to meet her early morning flight back to Pokhara. La Har also left us to meet his return bus to Pokhara. This journey would take him two days to complete. We would not see him again for another five days. Despite our best efforts, there was no room left on the small planned as we had planned to pay for his ticket too. With bags over our shoulders, we departed this lovely little town and set off for our first stop.

Despite the laid back life style in Nepal compared to our rushed lives, flights into and out of Jomsom are strictly adhered to. Smack bang on time, as we were walking down the valley, Kim's flight swooped over us as it zoomed away for Pokhara. By this time several flights had already preceded hers and the airways quickly became busy as the large number of flights rushed to deliver their passengers before the Mustang winds picked up around 11:00am. As a general rule on the use of electronic equipment whilst flying either don't exist or are widely ignored, Kim was able to film her take off. The runway is reported as being 531 metres long and according to Kim, the pilot used all of it. Her video clip clearly shows the end of the runway disappearing from under the wheels before the plane quickly climbs and banks to avoid the steeply rising mountains south of the end of the runway near Syang, our next destination.

It was in Syang (2,820 metres) that we were meeting the sister of Mangal, who we had met in Kathmandu. Her village had been trying to get a functioning health post up and running for some years. We had plenty of first aid bundles remaining that we had allocated for this purpose so we were disappointed to discover on our arrival that she had walked to Jomsom to meet us. We had crossed paths somewhere on the trail. How embarrassing! The boys found her home and we were greeted by a beautiful old woman in traditional dress who turned out to be her mother. Her grin from ear to ear told us how much she was enjoying having visitors. She was insistent that we stay for tea but as our day was going to be long, we sadly had to decline. Leaving the bundles of supplies with her, she then pressed some local apples on us for the journey. With big smiles on our faces and with much use of our broken Nepali, we thanked her for her generosity and took our leave. Walking through the village, I did spot a Red Cross post but it was tightly padlocked.

Bouncing down the trail, everything seemed to be easier now we were at low altitude. We wandered the trail down to Marpha past the army mountaineering school. The area is renowned for the fine apples that are grown there and for the Nilgiri Distillery. Mike and Margaret had told us all before that it was in Marpha that some of the best apple pies are made and that the apples are sent all over the country.

The valley had begun to narrow by this point but still the scale and width of the valley floor is difficult to describe. There are broad flats that weave around the rock outcrops. A road follows the walls on the east side which has brought an increase in both vehicular and pedestrian traffic. Overhead the constant sound of aircraft flying in and out of Jomsom combined with the diesel rumble of hulking Tata trucks in all their shining and painted finery, the plethora of buses prepared to brave the road, and sturdy Mahindra four-wheel drives. The air was warm and pleasant even though the clouds were heavy and expectant with rain.

As we hit the outskirts of Marpha, I was pleasantly surprised to find the wide paved laneways set with close fitting flag-stones. All the buildings presented with a form of whitewash. Everything was clean and regular rubbish bins could be seen along the lane way. A range of shop fronts dotted the sides. From underneath our feet came the sounds of running water. A lifted square of stone revealed a fast running drain along the length of the lane. Taps appeared at regular intervals where the residents could obtain clean, fresh water although we would still be required to treat it for drinking.

I was so enamoured by the town that I was just following the boys and had not realised that Margaret, Mike, and Sandra had headed off up a side lane. The building at which they ended up sat above the town at the top of a well-made staircase. It provided them with clear views over the flat roof tops to both the north and south. While I was filming, they caught up with me and we headed to a local establishment for morning tea. It was set back into the wall behind a bakery shop front. It turned out to also be a hotel with two storeys of rooms out a side door. We indulged ourselves with a slice of the local apple pie. Sandra and Margaret washed theirs down with a glass of apple lassi. It was really delicious with a crumbly short crust and lightly spiced with possibly cardamom and cinnamon. The room was bright and well lit with skylights but in the hot morning sun, the room felt a little stifling. It was clean and neat but quiet given that the trekking season tidal wave was still making its way up the Marsyangdi Nadi.

As we left Marpha, the winds had already picked up. It had become dusty and dirty while the walking became a bit of a hard slog for me. At least it was downhill. The temperature had become warm enough to raise sweat which just made the dirt stick in greater quantities.

We arrived at Tukuche (2,590 metres) which is a widely set out town. A hospital sits at a fork in the trail; its grounds green and lush with lots of open grass on which people could sit in the sun. Feeling much brighter now that our trail was primarily downhill or flat, I was beginning to focus more on the people passing me by. With a smile I would great each person with a "Namaste" to which they would either nod or answer me back with a smile. As I approached an elderly woman, out of respect, I greeted her and placed my hands, palms together, under my chin. This is the more formal way of doing things that the younger generations use less. Her face

181

split into a wide grin as she said "Namaste bibi" in reply. She chuckled as she kept going. My perplexed look and confusion was answered by Dhan who explained that bibi means nice young man. I laughed heartily at that, given my own age might not have been that much younger than hers.

We took a break in a hotel for some lemon tea. Stepping through the low doorway into the courtyard, we were confronted with a bright, airy space dotted with tables under umbrellas. Around and above us was the guest rooms of this establishment that we were advised had been in the one family for 150 years or more. To our left was the indoor dining room. From behind the glass counter the family smiled shyly at us; their stocks of cigarettes, films, batteries, alcohol, and even biscuits filling the space behind the glass front and top. A sign proclaimed access to STD and ISD phone calls. A woman sat on the stairs in the sun cuddling a Tibetan wildcat kitten. After a brief query through Dorje, she eventually permitted me to film the kitten playing in her lap. Ah the joy of kittens everywhere in the world stalking a piece of grass. Mike had some fun with Dorje and Kanchha that involved lifting them up so that a set of Yak horns rested on their heads.

Sadly we had to move on. The roads were starting to become busy with pedestrians. A lot of them were young. The local boarding schools had just finished for a period of school holidays. These students were now walking home for the break with school books in hand. In some cases, they would be walking for two days. Some were covering distances up to 80 kilometres in that time. All of them were well dressed and very polite. Dorje encouraged us to talk with them to help improve their English skills. We walked through the village of Kobang (2,560 metres) level with the river to our left. The scattering of buildings to our right sat behind a very narrow but fast flowing stream. A couple of kilometres away to the east on the other side of the river near the village of Sirkung, a landslide could be clearly seen against the hills. Dhan explained that a tea house had been buried when the earth moved but could not tell me if anyone had been killed.

The road undulated as it tried to stay above flood levels. Fields on our right were fenced off with dry stone walls and even had full height timber doors. Corn and apple groves were protected with barbed wire against predation from animals.

Our lunch stop was at Larjung (2,550 metres). To enter the main part of the village, we had to cross a fast flowing, rocky stream. As the normal path was mostly submerged, the boys attempted to rebuild the ford by dropping rocks into the water. Kanchha was trying his hardest to soak Dorje by throwing the biggest rocks he could into the stream bed.

Having climbed over the levee into the village, Dorje immediately called a halt to my progress. Pointing carefully at the low eaves of a house next to the path, he whispered "bees" where a swarm was moving in and out of a new hole in the wall. Apparently this was a new nest and the bees would be very, very protective. Taking charge of my video camera, he sent me on to give the spot a wide berth. The footage that he captured showed them quite clearly as they built the new hive.

Selecting a hotel for lunch, we quickly discovered that a majority of the school kids had selected the same venue. They had taken over one floor while we were given another room nearby. A cast iron pot sat on the floor under the table. This would normally be lit in winter to keep the diners warm. A similar one had been under the table at Hotel Alka Mar-Copolo in Jomsom. The kids had access to a TV and were apparently watching some form of talent show similar to Indian Idol or even Euro Vision. The announcer could be heard giving out the voting number for voice and text votes. As some of the more popular songs came on, the kids could all be heard singing along with the performers. A passing student was waylaid by Mike who wanted to ask him some questions about the boy's obviously traditionally made khukuri. The young man was happy to show off his blade. A couple of the grade 10 girls shyly joined us as they wanted to conduct a tourism survey. After answering their questions about why we had come and what we hoped to see, they were happy to answer a few questions themselves. We wanted to know what their hopes and dreams were. One girl wanted to study overseas so that she could learn new skills that she could bring back to Nepal to improve their lives. Her wish was to study as a teacher in America, Australia, Europe, or India. Unlike some kids, this young lady did not want to remain overseas. Rather she wanted to gather the latest information to improve everyone's life at home. Such a wise head on her shoulders, I did not want to suggest she might decide to stay in the bright lights of the wider world. Her enthusiasm for her own country was such a positive message in such a poor country.

On the south end of Larjung we encountered one girl who was limping. A friend was helping by carrying her bag but it was clear she was in trouble. After asking permission, Mike and I checked her feet and discovered a mass of blisters on the back of both heels. We patched her up as best we could and seriously considered paying her bus fare all the way home but she declined with a shy smile.

The road was again following the river with the occasional diversion because of side streams joining the Kali Gandaki. On reaching the Sun Khola, we were advised to follow the road inland to the La Thau Temple where a modern metal foot bridge crossed the river near where a new road bridge was being constructed. All the students and a fair number of other trekkers had elected to cross directly at the mouth of the side river. This was a dangerous move as we had been told this river will claim at least one life every year in the swollen, fast moving waters. Despite the fact we had walked a much longer distance, we still managed to beat the majority of those who had taken the direct route. Back up on to the road, we found the young girl with blisters who had reached her pain threshold. At that point we offered to pay the fare and insist she take the bus however her friend told the boys the ticket had already been bought. Her remaining journey would be in the bumpy relative comfort of a local bus... whenever it eventually arrived.

South of the Sun Khola, we crossed a bridge to the east side of the Kali Gandaki where we were now on what was described as the winter road and relatively easy going. Passing through Kokhethanti, Dhampu and Satsaya we eventually crossed over to the west bank again as we entered the town of Kalapani (2,530 metres). The roads were wide and constructed of crushed rock. Various vehicles were heading up and down the road requiring us to step to the side. Kalapani has a major school for tertiary level studies. The courses listed at the front gate included tourism and catering, and the relatively rare veterinary sciences. Just down the road was a large school, perhaps as large as a lot of city high schools in Australia in terms of grounds. Stone walls facing the road also doubled as tiered seating for two full-sized volleyball courts on the lowest terrace. Playing on those would be hard work as the surface was fine gravel.

Directly next door was the neat and clean establishment of the See You Hotel. Set in a 'U' shape, this two-storey structure held a series of comfortable rooms each with their own ensuite. Perhaps the hardest part was the metal staircase where each tread was much higher than the average tread height. This meant an extra-large step for already wobbly legs to be negotiated going up and a big drop when descending. On the left side of the 'U' was the dining room and substantial kitchen. A truck had arrived and was unloading foam boxes labelled fresh fish. It seemed that they had gone to the expense of importing fish rather than obtaining any from the river. I was not certain they could easily obtain the required quantities. From what I had been told, students from the hospitality school just up the road would work there to develop their skills.

The rooms were comfortable and spacious. Lots of light came in through the windows creating a pleasant, almost home-like experience. The beds were more modern in their construction but still a trifle hard. Of all things though after a hard days walking and feeling dirty and slimy, I just wanted a shower. Disrobing and stepping into the generous tiled bathroom I discovered that there was no hot water. Braving myself, I turned on the cold water and gingerly eased myself into the chilly waters for a scrubbing. After a few minutes of this invigorating experience, I dived out and briskly towelled myself dry. It wasn't the most pleasant shower that I had taken but I'd already had a few cold showers on this journey and at least I was clean. Dressing in some warmer layers, I stepped out onto the balcony so that I could secure my room and head down for evening meal. It was at that point that Mike, I think it was, shouted up to me that hot water was working in the other half of the hotel and that they had opened a room for us to go over and shower. Cursing the poor timing and the fates under my breath, I politely declined and gingerly made my way back down the stair case. Sandra later reported that the shower was tepid at best.

By this stage my calves were pumped up to an almost painful state from all the walking down hill and the pace that we had maintained all day. A check of the map showed that we had covered an amazing 23 kilometres that day although we had only descended around 185 vertical metres. Margaret remembers this as "a very hard, long day!"

With aching muscles I joined the others at a large rectangular table where we enjoyed a beer or two to celebrate the days' achievement. On the wall in the corner of the room, a television had been turned on. I sat dazed and enthralled watching programs I could barely understand. For me the withdrawal symptoms suddenly returned and it didn't matter what was on, it was the news in fact, as long as I could just see a little of the idiot box. Tired as I was, I hung on long enough to eat my meal, update my diary, and prepare the next blog entry before retiring for the night.

We were all tired, and Sandra was in bed by 7:30, although she didn't sleep as well as hoped given the students partying through the night with drums and singing.

I knew only too well that at about 06:00 there would be a knock on the door as the boys brought around that joyous cup of 'bed tea.' This ritual had been very welcome each day since the start of the trek. Each morning, the boys would come around to each room and wake us with a cup of strong, hot black tea, a bowl of large granule sugar on the tray beside the cups.

It was a restful night's sleep even though the bed was again on the hard side. Already the sun was up and the town was beginning to bustle. A local police unit travelled north by four-wheel drive presumably on patrol. The day was overcast but decidedly warm.

Rain promised to be somewhere in the vicinity based on the humidity we could feel. Shouldering our day bags we set off knowing that tonight would have a treat in store. Again generally this was all downhill. By common acknowledgement, the Kali Gandaki gorge is considered the deepest gorge in the world coming in at over five and a half kilometres from the highest peak to lowest point. This leads to a focussing of weather patterns in the area.

As the road began a rise up away from the river, the relatively gentle climb began to really hurt. Legs already pumped up were beginning to become painful. My hips had begun to ache again, a feeling I had not had for a few days. The sensation was of impending rain that, in Australia, warns me of a change some days away. Kim often jokes that my artificial hips made me an excellent human barometer. In Nepal, I noted, the timeframe could be as little as 40 minutes. What it proved was the clouds were coming down as we climbed higher. For a while we walked along a flat section of road while around us a wall of white drifted up slope. Visibility was less than 200 metres. During a rare opening in the cloud cover, I could see a giant landslip on the other side of the gorge which extended from above us all the way down to the turbulent waters hundreds of metres below.

As the cover began to thin and break, we stopped for a break outside a stone house. A shy young girl sat on the roof of the house glancing sideways at the foreigners. The owner's Tibetan Mastiff had taken an interest in our group as they are known to do. With his cattle bell clanging as he walked, we drew his attention for over an hour before he got bored and left us. I was advised that there have been recorded examples of these guard dogs following trekkers upwards of three days before returning home. At home this might be considered 'cute' but when a dog capable of killing a bear takes an interest in you, it can be most disconcerting. Yes they are cute and worthy of a respectful pat but you just don't know what is going through their mind.

Approaching Ghasa (2,010 metres) we were going to have to wait while Dorje had our trekking permits stamped at the local police post so we planned on having morning tea here. Wandering through the village, Sandra and I picked up another Tibetan Mastiff. While we sat waiting for Dorje, the mastiff came and sat heavily on my foot. I know that move very well. Tentatively I reached out and began to scratch around the ear through the thick pelt. The eyes began to roll up as the dog succumbed to the joy of human contact. From the sounds of wonder from the local kids, I gathered that this might be a rare event when a foreigner is brave enough to touch so savage an animal. Juggling the video camera in one hand, I managed to capture the look of contentment on the black and tan muzzle. One that I would gladly have taken home was it even remotely possible.

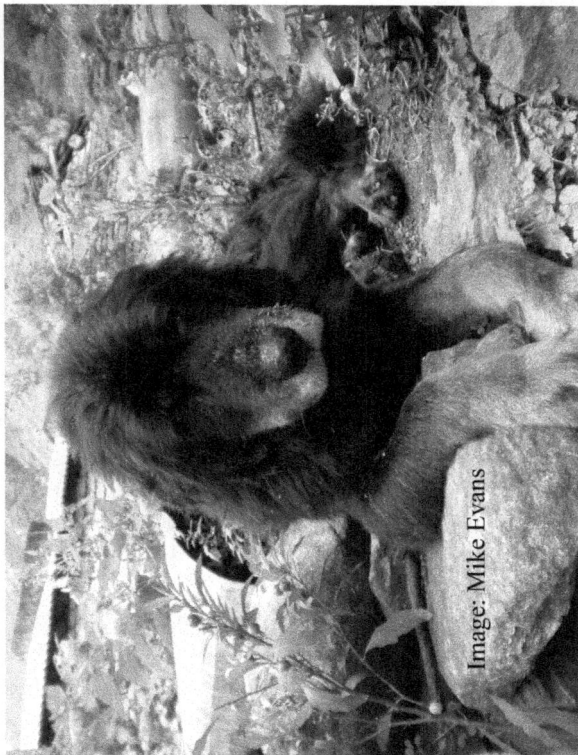

Image: Mike Evans

An older gentleman with a series of wire baskets on his back full of lollies, fairy-floss and wafer shapes full of powdered sherbet set his load down nearby. He was immediately pestered by the local kids looking for something cheap to buy. As Dorje returned, we said goodbye to our canine companion and continued a bit further down the road where we stopped for morning tea.

Out the front of the tea house was the ambulance from further north up the gorge at Lete which immediately drew my attention. My interest was purely professionally motivated and not related to my usual sticky-beaking at fellow emergency services, I promise you. As the vehicle was occupied, I tried to be discrete but it was possible to see a bench seat down either side of the back of the four-wheel drive. Both seats were covered in a white sheet. A bottle of oxygen was strapped in behind the driver and a set of metal shelves held some basic dressings. From the way people seemed to be climbing on and off, it seemed they were using it as a taxi rather than an ambulance.

Our host in the tea house hobbled out to greet us with a crutch under one arm. Mike and I offered to re-strap his ankle as it was causing him quite some discomfort and he could not afford to stay off it. He was the main source of income for his family so we could only advise him to stay off it whenever he could. His wife and daughter posed for a photo with Margaret at the back of the dining room. Out the front she managed to spot a brand new children's bicycle so new that it didn't even appear to have been used.

As we prepared to depart, Dorje brought me a young boy with some long term wounds on his arm. While they were not bleeding, they did not appear to be healing. Unsure of what we were the doing, Dorje reassured the boy, while I checked him over. The best option I had in my kit was a spray on skin product which also provided a form of antiseptic. In acknowledgement of the stoicism of the Nepali, the boy did not even flinch as I sprayed the product on. From personal experience and with my high tolerance for pain, I know that it really stings. With some advice from Dorje to not touch the area and to let the spray set, we caught up with everyone else on the road.

Both Margaret and I were beginning to feel the trail again so the plan was to get a jeep to Tatopani. At the boundaries between districts, I was told, the equivalent of a bus depot exists where vehicles used for passenger transport swap their loads. This is apparently a way to ensure that income from passengers is shared between drivers from different districts. A conversation ensued to secure passage for the two of us, some of the boys and all the bags. The final price was overheard by another driver who began to argue that we were being charged too much. Other drivers chimed in that because we were foreigners we could afford more and should be charged as such. The next we knew, there was a massive argument involving every spare driver. Ok, I'm all for free enterprise and drivers getting a fair price for a service offered but this rapidly spiralled out of control. The next thing we knew, every passenger on every vehicle was being thrown off their buses and four-wheel drives. With confusion clearly written on our faces, the boys explained that the drivers had gone on strike over the whole issue of pricing. Nobody was travelling in either direction. Dorje liaised with Mike and directed us to carry on walking. One four-wheel drive soon passed us with many of the drivers piled on board as they headed down the valley to the district administration office to argue their points of view. My understanding was that it took half a day to resolve the issue. Shaking my head, we carried on until we reached Thaplyang.

Two girls and a boy met us on the road offering green looking citrus for sale. Apparently this type of orange is edible but naturally sour. Sandra managed to get a photo with them. Here Mike and Sandra elected to cross the river at the suspension bridge to follow the old trekking trail on the east bank. Given the struggles Margaret and I were having, it was suggested that we cover the next stretch on the new road of the west bank. Purna and Dhan stayed with us for this stretch.

Once again the warm weather was mixed with the ominous heavy dark clouds looming over head. Distant rumbles could occasionally be heard over the ever present river. Along the way, Purna pointed out a large waterfall that he called "Beautiful Waterfall" and it definitely was that. Some of the other trekkers with whom we were often crossing paths had stopped to enjoy the chilling waters. We elected not to join them although one Spanish guy had convinced his girlfriend to climb under the waters so he could take some photos of her. While it was hard to be certain, my map suggested this water was falling from high above as the Rupse Khola. It was just around the next bend that we stopped for lunch in a small village of Rupse (1,630 metres).

In a rare oversight, it seemed that the tea houses and lodges there were not yet ready for tourists and it took about an hour for two omelettes to arrive. While very late in making the table, the portions, as always, were generous and we enjoyed listening to the river as we ate. Were it not for the sound, we would not have known the river was below us as the vegetation was very thick. We had hoped that the others would meet us here so we could finish the run down to Tatopani.

With a few spots of rain beginning to fall, we moved quickly back up onto the road just in time for a tropical storm to come pounding down. While struggling into our coats, we became thoroughly soaked. In my haste, I had grabbed my coat and not my poncho and despite my day pack having its own cover, the side of the pack against my coat was soon dripping. This meant that when the rain passed, I still had the cloying dampness of the pack pressed up against me. Mind you, coats and ponchos in this environment only kept the rain off, they did nothing for the humidity and immediate sweating which became just as bad as standing in the rain. Margaret, quite rightly, elected to forgo the poncho as it really provided no benefit and just increased the amount of heat against the body.

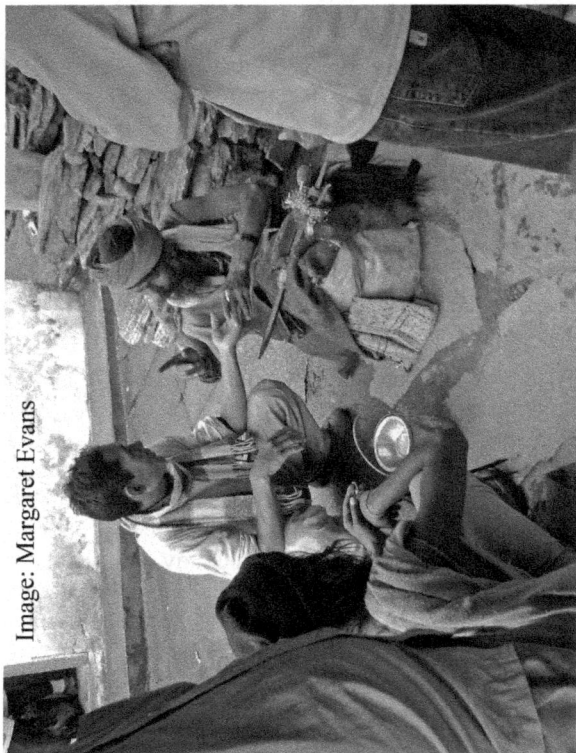

Image: Margaret Evans

Several minutes later, as we passed another lodge beside the road, a whistle shrilled out at us from under the veranda. Kanchha was standing under cover with his ever present grin. Somehow we had missed the others and they had holed up waiting for the rain to pass or at least ease off. As we caught up with Mike and Sandra, the boys sat chatting and sharing cigarettes with a Brahmin sadhu or mystic.

Their track was much more undulating than ours, which they could see from time to time through the trees. They stopped for tea at a small village where the locals were very involved in playing a game on a table top that involved flicking small tokens across the surface. The villages on their side of the river were much less prosperous. The children were dirty and had runny noses. They had obviously missed the benefits of the tourist trade. There were houses and restaurants standing deserted after the trade had gone with the new road.

Mike suggested that since the new road had opened, trekkers rarely used the old trails and so money had dried up. Formerly immaculately kept stone paths had begun to collapse. Buildings, long since abandoned, had begun to fall into disrepair. They reported seeing a young girl of perhaps 14 years of age heavily pregnant. There was nowhere that they had seen where accommodation could now be found; such a sad state of affairs as a result of something so simple as a road. As the rain lifted, we carried on down the road where we concluded day 15 at Tatopani (1,190 metres).

Our stop for the night was the appropriately named Trekker's Lodge & Restaurant where sadly, once again, we were out of hot water. But for once it wasn't an issue. Tatopani is famous for natural hot springs. For a reasonable Rs40 ($AU0.43), you can soak your cares away in these large square pools at the same level as the river rushing past nearby. If I remember correctly they were open from 05:00 AM until about 10:00 PM. Several masseurs offer their skills and with the right amount of rupee, you can be served food and drink at the edge of the pool. The only requirement is that you have to wash down with soap and water before you get in. This is no hardship since the water is tapped straight off the pools, nice and hot. Sore muscles at the end of a long day deserve this treatment.

Of course if anything was going to happen to someone in the group, it had to be me. While descending the steps to the washing area, my sandals slipped on the soap covered stones and I landed squarely on my butt. Several locals immediately came to my aid and while I wasn't injured, judging by the good natured laughing around me, I had provided the afternoon's entertainment.

Having walked 20 kilometres and descended 1,335 metres, we had earned our soak. Lazing there for around an hour, we returned to the lodge for our evening meal. A mother and daughter from North Stradbroke in Queensland were on the next table with their male companion from Belgium. Like many trekkers they had arrived in Kathmandu with little equipment or knowledge of trekking and had opted not to have a guide or porter. Mike showed them how to carry a backpack to reduce back pain. They were heading up the valley to Jomsom so we shared tales over a lovely meal and a beer or two.

With a delicious chicken steak in my belly, it was time to retire in preparation for the next day's climb.

Chapter 10 - What? More up?

"If you reject the food, ignore the customs, fear the religion and avoid the people, you might better stay home." - James Michener

Taken from my diary on the 22nd of September:

> "Homesickness finally setting [in] after a text from the girls that I found this morning. How funny that even a message that your cat is missing you can be so powerful."

Somehow all the expended energy of the last few days combined with the lack of sleep came crashing down. I was missing Kim, missing home and missing my furry kids. The cats, dog, horses, chooks, ducks, geese and doves form an important part of my life. Despite being in a group of wonderful friends, both Australian and Nepali, I felt alone. Sometimes when you trek, you trek alone because it's your one foot in front of another. Nobody else can do it for you. To be missing home can make that loneliness even stronger. But I was still living a great adventure; one that was soon coming to an end, which saddened me too.

But first there was 'a little bit up' to go. With most of the boys missing somewhere, we set off from Tatopani. Crossing the Kali Gandaki and the Ghar Khola on the swaying suspension bridges, of which I was no longer apprehensive, at Gharkholagaon, we began a steep switchback climb into the hills again. On the first steep stretch, we passed a man with a woven basket seat on his back. In the seat sat a wizened old woman facing outwards. Her stoic expression suggested to me that she was probably ill since not even a 'Namaste' could rouse her interest. The boys said she was being taken to the doctor.

We were attempting to follow the old trekking route but even here, progress has made its mark. Time and again we would either walk on or cross over the same brand new road that had been pushed up the hill. After days of 'a little bit down', this seemed more like 'Nepali up' then 'Aussie up.' Every step of mine seemed a struggle while the likes of Mike and Sandra relished the new experience, seizing it with the same enthusiasm that had marked every other day for them. Before long the sun came out and the humidity went through the roof. I quickly became soaked under my day pack. What little breeze found its way to us did little to ease the discomfort. Mike's portable weather station showed that the temperature was about 22 degrees but with the high humidity, it felt much hotter.

Despite that, or perhaps because of it, we took opportunities to enjoy the views and watch the small farms being worked as we passed by. Stopping under the shade of some trees in the bend of the road, we heard a shout from above. A water buffalo had decided to make its own path and was trotting down the road towards us with its owner in hot pursuit. We quickly formed a human barrier and the water buffalo stopped, confounded by this new obstacle and not sure that it wanted to test it out. With many 'dhanyabads' (thank you), the farmer took possession of his valuable charge and turned it back to his field for the day's work.

During another rest break, several young children came running down the road past us, laughing and giggling in the way of kids all over the world. Stopping nearby, they squatted in the rock on the edge of the new road and began sorting through and chipping away at some of the stones. I was enthralled by their actions.

Making an assumption, I thought they must have been children of a stone mason who were practicing their new trade. How wrong I was. We all smiled when we realised that they were chipping selected stones into wheels which they would roll down the road. Having seen how far that one had rolled, they would make another one and repeat the process.

Leaving them to their game, we continued our ascent. Sometimes using the road and sometimes following the boys as they would climb narrow but well used trails into the almost jungle-like growth that we had not really seen for a fortnight. The vegetation was open with thick undergrowth but where we broke out into open ground, often a very short grass almost like a bowling green was growing in the sunlight.

At one point, I'm not entirely sure where, I stopped to film a baby goat bouncing around with the joy of being in the sun. The doe quietly enjoyed her meal next to a small but fast moving stream as her kid enjoyed life in general. The video recorded my giggle of joy, or was that hysteria, at this simple pleasure of life. However one moment the kid was in my view finder, the next it had disappeared. With cries of distress, I noticed that it had fallen backwards in between some rocks and was slowly but inevitably sliding into the water. Cutting the recording, I raced across someone's field and just managed to grab the kid by the scruff of the neck. Dragging it rather unceremoniously to safety, it bleated at me before bouncing off again to its mother. The doe munched a few times, looked at me, seemed to sigh "kids" and went back to eating.

Finally we broke out of the jungle onto the road which gave us a relatively consistent surface to walk on. By now, most of the boys had caught up to us. Several hundred metres later as we reached the highest point, the boys disappeared down a side trail behind a pile of rocks and earth where a little tea house was perched on the edge overlooking to the Ghar Khola. Settling onto the comfortable bench seats, we enjoyed the view over a cup of tea. The shop front was wire mesh with all the products stacked up on view. A small child of maybe two or three years of age played peek-a-boo with me from inside the shop. She giggled a lot but never fully appeared in view preferring to peer out from behind tins of fruit juice, plastic bottles of soft drink, packets of cigarettes and coconut biscuits.

Two men good naturedly argued and bickered as they worked manually on the road side. Lifting and balancing large rocks to form the road verge, often they were but one step from sliding several hundred metres down through the loose surface. Occasionally, they would over balance a large rock which would slip and tumble its way down into the valley below, crashing into the edge of the jungle. And so the bickering would begin again. It was hot work in the now glaring sun.

A small kitten tentatively appeared from amongst the rocks and began to gnaw on the wrist strap of my walking pole. In the rapidly heating sun, its play became more and more acrobatic. Human contact was limited to occasional smooching of fingers stretched in its direction but holding and cuddles were out of the question.

Approaching from the direction we would eventually walk, an English woman and her Iranian husband joined us at the tea shop. Under the shade of the awning, she told us how they had been to Nepal some twenty years previously. The changes she had seen, she said, had saddened her as there had been a loss of culture with the increased vehicular access. Towns she had seen had changed beyond all recognition as populations had ebbed and flowed. They had travelled the old trail all the way to Jomsom previously and were hoping to do it again.

Wishing them well, we shouldered our packs for the next stretch. This part became gentler as we crossed the slope rather than climbed. Dhan had pointed across the valley to a collection of buildings in the distance and said that we would stop there for the night. Part of the walk was in the open and my consumption of water began to go up. Eventually our path had us threading our way through the cooling trees. A slight breeze made things somewhat more comfortable.

As I rounded a corner, the others had settled in to a small stand beside the path. A young man was selling fresh curd by the glass so we settled in to enjoy. This was so fresh it had been made that morning. No flavours had been added and despite the slight acidity, it was rather lovely. Mike engaged the young man in an extended conversation comparing farming methods in Nepal and Australia. Dorje and Dhan were having a hard time keeping up the translating. Apparently he had six water buffalo which meant that he had some wealth. If memory serves me correctly, one cow is about NPR16,000 or $AU172 at the current rates. Since the average wage is about $US240 per year, he had done a very good job.

Reluctantly we continued on our way. Not far down the track, Margaret and Sandra encountered two young girls sitting at their parent's tea house doing their homework. Sandra observed that the children in Nepal love their schooling. Even though it was school holiday time, the children are always dedicated to their studies. Since both of them had a background in teaching, they had a quick chat with the girls about their English homework. A sign on the outside of the tea house listed some of the countries from which passing travellers had hailed. Even though the written English was somewhat corrupted, they had done a good job spelling each country phonetically and you could easily determine what each one was.

On one stretch of the path, Margaret met a woman with her crying child in her arms. Calling the boys over, she discovered that the child was running a fever. Sorting through our meagre first aid supplies, we got some paracetamol for her and made up a small packet to hold it. With very strict instructions on its usage and suggestion that she see the doctor soon, dutifully translated by Dorje and Dhan, we left her with the wishes that her child would get better soon.

The inevitable finally came to pass and we once again had to deal with steps. Up and up we climbed. My thighs burned with the effort. The stairs were all well-constructed but the constant up was an effort. Finally we arrived in the village of Shikha (1,935 metres) at 13:30 and I was pleasantly surprised to be informed that this was the end of the day's walking.

Shikha is a lovely little village with stone paving throughout. It supports a reasonably good sized school which I could see from my room's window. A joint country jungle warfare school is located somewhere nearby. The surrounding landscape showed small farms dotted across the cleared landscape. From my room, I could see a recent large landslide several kilometres away. A small dwelling perched precariously near the top edge of the wounded hill.

Our lodgings had hot water by both solar and electric means and we availed ourselves of this luxury. Feeling much refreshed, some clothes washing was in order and with some bowls supplied by the owner, we retreated to the roof for some scenic laundry work. As many items as we thought might dry in time were given the soap and water treatment. Lines were strung across the roof already so everything was hung up to drip dry. In some cases, flat surfaces already hot from the sun were used as both dryer and iron.

Traditionally, when the washing is done, the water is not wasted but thrown on the vegetable garden. So this is what I did. Only to discover my bar of clothes washing soap was still in the water and it sailed over the side of the building, down five storeys into the broccoli below.

With much embarrassment on my part, and gales of laughter on the owner's part, I explained my predicament and she guided me down through the building's basement and into the garden. Retrieving my soap, I was able give the garden a once over. A wide range of vegetables were being grown from corn to broccoli, leafy greens to beans, more than enough food to feed guests at this hotel. The basement room was piled to the ceiling with potatoes and had that cool, musty/earthy smell common to such places.

In the doorway of the hotel attached to a door pillar was a back brace loom. Currently using it was the grandmother or great grandmother of the household but every woman would take their turn as they produced sturdy textiles. The current project was about 30 or 40 centimetres wide and about one and a half metres long in bright traditional colours. By leaning forward, the warp fibres would be relaxed to let the shuttle pass through. A wooden rod would be used to keep the thread straight. By leaning back, tension would be applied to the material.

As the sun started its drift towards the horizon, it was noticeably cooler and we brought the damp washing inside as the humidity began to build. The owner kindly lit the wood fire in the dining room where ropes were strung to hang such clothing. Amongst our prayer flags made up of t-shirts, trekking pants and underwear, we quietly read, updated diaries and chatted amiably with some Indian gentlemen who we had seen up at Thorung La.

The television had been switched on, and after a non-descript movie we were surprised to find Australian factual series "Bondi Rescue" showing. Everyone was feeling tired and our packs seemed heavier each day, but that away from the new road and on the old trail, it was so much quieter and peaceful.

As night descended, having eaten our meal and exhaustion beginning to set in, we retreated for the night to our rooms. Guest houses and lodges along the major trails often have solid frames and outer walls. When it comes to internal structures, however, often walls are put up quickly to get them ready for customers. Consequently we noted that often the internal walls were made of five-ply laminated sheets similar to packing crate material. From time to time, you might even be afforded the luxury of insulation like in Chame where thin packing foam had been placed in-between the wall studs. They would be comparatively cheap to build and cover large areas quickly, but they did nothing to mask the sounds of my exhausted snoring or the spitting coming from the room of our neighbours.

With sun-up the next morning, came the regulation 'bed tea' served with sunny smiles all round. I didn't have much stomach for breakfast but tried to eat something. It was probably eggs and chapatti's but I really don't remember. Sandra remembers having porridge with apple. Her diary records that the humidity was already high in the early morning.

Leaving Shikha at 07:10, we began the day with a steep climb up stone stairs set in the side of the hill. The 'up' had definitely become Nepali again and I needed many stops along the way. Mike obviously needed to open up his legs and had quickly disappeared from view with Kanchha at his heels. It would be over an hour before we saw him again at Chitre (2,390 metres). In fact we were quite concerned about him, was he lost?

Along the way, we had waved to the locals and chatted with one man weaving a basket. He proudly told us the number of cattle he owned and asked where we were from. He nodded sagely when we said Australia. His English was excellent and his home orderly. I surmised he was probably a retired Ghurkha soldier.

The morning had become really steamy and it sapped the energy from me. Rest stops became more and more regular but were kept short as the leeches were coming out everywhere. They sense the body heat and you only need to stop for a few minutes and they will be inching towards you. Well me, anyway. Kim normally draws the mosquitos but I seem to be a leech magnet.

209

Eventually we reached Chitre and stopped in the grounds of a lovely hotel with well-manicured lawns for a drink. Mountain peaks were popping out of the surrounding clouds and we enjoyed the views they afforded. Bright flowers lined the boundaries of the lawn and large black and blue butterflies danced amongst them on the gentle warm breeze. In a small field just below us, baby goats pranced in the sun. To our left, back down the path, I noticed a small hospital. Its gates were closed and locked, the curtains drawn. Dhan explained that the hospital had been closed for many months as no doctor could be found to run it, a sad state of affairs.

Heading on up the path, a few minutes later we found Mike at another lodge, New Annapurna Lodge & Restaurant, where he had chosen to stop and wait for us. He said that he had been waiting an hour for us to catch up with a grin on his face. This lodge also had a flat lawn area where the boys were playing soccer with some of the local kids. Occasionally there would be a cry as the ball would be lost bouncing down the path and someone would have to chase after it, just in case it found its way back to Tatopani.

A high framework covered with thick thatch protected cobs of corn drying in the sun. The thatch keeps the rain off while the high frame stops rodents and wildlife from gaining a free meal.

Image: Mike Evans

More climbing followed and we met up again with the Sydney doctor and his wife along the way. Eventually we arrived at Ghorepani (2,860 metre) at 11:50. Our shortest day yet, we climbed up past many hotels. Each one looked a lovely proposition but we kept walking. Entering a broad area in the centre of town, Dorje cut down a narrow alley between several buildings which popped out into a large open area with many volleyball courts attached to a school.

At the other end of this space sat The Sunny Hotel. With a large naturally lit dining room, this hotel is run by Captain Dam Bahadur Pun, retired, with all the military precision of his Ghurkha training. An efficient team worked the well-ordered kitchen. The rooms were clean and neat, if somewhat basic and were named after world famous athletes and mountaineers. Sandra slept in the 'Tiger Woods' room, but unfortunately I can't remember what mine was called. Hot water was plentiful and the wine selection somewhat extensive. Captain Pun and his wife were friendly and welcoming. Large windows on three walls give magnificent views of the Annapurna range peaks which, when we arrived, were poking through thick cloud. During a chat with our host, it was soon revealed that Captain Pun had also been a Commonwealth Games diving competitor, having been trained in India.

While our day was short, the push up the mountain had been hard. I was exhausted and really needed a break. The boys had wandered off to enjoy their short day of work. Margaret and Sandra had headed out to do some much-needed retail therapy. Mike was chatting with Captain Pun and his wife about their son in the British Ghurkha regiment. I sat in the dining room updating my diary, half listening to Mike's conversation.

Captain Pun was talking about the health post in Ghorepani. He was part of a local association consisting of the hotel owners. Every year they would donate a percentage of their income towards funding the project. A German doctor provided clinical support and visited on a semi regular basis. I became more intrigued and sat in on the conversation for a while. Having heard all about the health post, I decided it might be worth the supreme effort to find the building and have a look for myself.

Girding my aching legs, I headed out past the volleyball courts. Ahh here was where the boys had headed to after playing a game of chess. They were engaged in a porters versus trekkers match which involved more laughing and chasing after lost balls than actual game. I had no idea what the score was or where they even found the energy but they were enjoying themselves. Volleyball seems to be widely played and just about every school we had seen had at least one court.

Knowing we had not passed the health post I figured it must be further along through the town. Stepping out of the narrow laneway into the small central square of Ghorepani, I turned left at the bakery and began walking along the smoothly paved square. Local music was playing from a nearby store. Everything was overcast but comfortably warm. Chickens scavenged for scraps in the street.

The path began to head down the hill and internally I groaned, knowing I would have to climb this again on my return. After a few minutes of descending steps, there was a nagging feeling that I might have missed the health post. Deciding it was best to ask for help, I stepped over to the nearby police post. A young man in neatly pressed uniform eyed me suspiciously before politely enquiring in broken English what I was after. "Health Post," I said. Looking at me quizzically while he tried to decipher what I had said, he eventually looked sympathetic. Apparently assuming I was another traveller afflicted with a dodgy belly, he directed me further down the hill and, nodding once, he returned to his duty.

With a sigh, I continued down the hill. This was obviously going to hurt when I returned. But eventually I located the post. Opposite a two-storey hotel and surrounded by beautifully kept gardens with a front hedge of glaring marigolds was a U-shaped building painted white with blue trimmings. Up several steps I went, along the flat path. On either side, manicured grass lawns ran from the front fence up to the main building. Given the growth rate in this part of the world, someone was obviously kept fully employed just maintaining control of it all. I stepped up onto the concrete steps and approached the open door in the centre of the building.

Image: Ian Stanley-Eyles

The consulting room was clean and neat. To my right was an examination table with a curtain on an overhead rail. In the corner of the room, on a trolley, a D-sized oxygen cylinder with a therapy mask sat hanging ready for use. For the non-medical reader, a D-sized cylinder holds 1,500 litres of compressed oxygen. An older style wheel chair sat beside it. An orderly wooden desk was in the centre of the room with chairs on either side. Information brochures and a donations box were placed on it. To my left the entire wall was filled with medications and supplies. This was a very well set out facility, except that there was no one about.

A faint, enquiring "Hello?" came from behind me and I turned to see a young woman approaching along the path. Her name was Binu Thapa and she was the nurse assigned to the post. She had been sitting in the hotel over the road and had seen me walk up to the building so came rushing up to see if I was okay. The change that came over her face when I explained to her that I wasn't sick but wanted to see how everything worked was priceless. She inflated with pride. A broad grin breaking out on her face, she took me on a tour of the facility.

Over the next hour she showed me over the complex including a store room and an office space in one wing. The office, at that point, was empty apart from pictures stuck on the wall of visits by medical professionals and the German doctor who sponsors the post.

Proudly she pointed to a picture of two western women telling me that they were nurses and had stayed for a month. Having worked in Pokhara with a dentist, they had then come to Ghorepani and during the month conducted outreach clinics to nearby villages. They had performed many dental extractions, a big issue in the more remote parts of Nepal. But more importantly, she explained, they had dealt with an insidious problem. Many local women suffer from a prolapsed uterus and rarely seek medical attention. These nurses had been able to perform a simple fix for many of them and resolved the issue for the ones they had been able to speak with. Binu explained that one woman had put up with the problem for over 20 years.

In the other wing of the building, she showed me a basic three-bed ward which was currently unoccupied. Once the trekking season became busy, she said it would often have two or three people in it. Next to it was a rudimentary kitchen.

We sat in the consulting room and chatted about the numbers and types of cases she would see. Opening a medical register, Binu pointed to different medical conditions. There were a lot of gastro-intestinal issues and respiratory complaints from locals. Compared to trekking season, the work was steady but as visitors came through, stomach bugs, dental problems, blood pressure and Altitude Sickness problems were widely apparent.

Having had a wonderful time talking about many things, sadly I had to head back to the hotel for the evening meal. We exchanged email addresses and I left a 1,000 rupee note in the donations box.

I began the surprisingly steep climb back up the steps. My legs burned but I moved with more energy than I thought possible. Arriving back in the dining room, I found the others enjoying the view. The clouds had lifted and we could see the peaks blushed orange as the sun began its evening descent. Mike was engaged in a conversation with a porter whose English was not good but in his ineffable style, Mike soon had the young man smiling. Apparently he had been engaged by two trekkers and was being treated poorly. He had to carry both their packs and he was often ignored.

Whilst becoming less common, this practice still occurs by less than pleasant individuals (I've left the expletives out here) who either won't spend the money for proper support, don't think they'll need more porters, don't budget properly or who just don't care.

In the kitchen, an efficient team of men could be seen bustling around the stoves and preparation benches. Meals appeared with military precision and in generous portions. The room began to fill with trekkers and the buzz of the nightly sharing of tales in much the same manner as travellers all over the world. Rounds of drinks were shared and tired laughter trickled across the room. Behind the bar sat a collection of wine bottles. With some surprise, I noted a bottle of Grange Hermitage of a recent vintage resting on the shelves. How such an expensive bottle of wine had managed to find its way to Ghorepani was a mystery. Since the going rate is between $AU550-650 (research suggests this is the current going rate for a bottle of that age), it was a rare treasure to see and probably cost Captain Pun considerably more to bring to such a remote destination.

With the clouds having partly lifted, we ate our evening meal to the view of the nearby peaks stained in rose colours while the sun went down. My eyes were struggling to stay open as we discussed the plan to catch sunrise on Poon Hill nearby. It would mean another 04:30 start to the day. I had already made the decision to pass on the walk despite knowing I would be missing one of the finest views of the district.

Our nightly order of freshly boiled water in our own bottles was ready and I gathered mine to head to bed. Holding on to its loop top, I was unprepared for the excruciating pain as the bottle separated from the stopper. A one kilogram aluminium bottle falling just over one metre and landing on its edge, and wearing just my walking sandals for their end-of-day comfort meant that my big toenail took the full brunt of the impact. Even my high tolerance for pain was stretched to the limit but I managed to limp to bed and settle in for the night. Fortunately I was not splashed with the scalding water and barely lost any when the stopper came out.

Not surprisingly, my night was somewhat restless even with some pain relief on board and the sounds of some of the other guests continually clearing their throats. Around 04:00 I was woken by the sound of a heavy tropical downpour. Part of my befuddled mind realised that with rain like that, no one would be doing the climb to Poon Hill. As my eyes closed again, there was no small amount of disappointment. Since I was already awake, I probably would have gone too.

Promptly at 06:30, the regular knock came at the door for 'bed tea.' The morning routine of packing bags and getting ready for breakfast had become an efficient process. After taking breakfast, Captain Pun's wife approached us. With sincere apologies for our having missed the morning walk, she presented each of us with a copy of the panoramic photo taken from the lookout. These we carefully rolled, wrapped in plastic and stowed in our packs.

The Captain himself joined us and talked more about the health post and its support; how the two visiting nurses had travelled around and had raised NPR140,000 for the project while other donations were accepted in a range of currencies. The local hoteliers would make a collective donation each year to the running expenses. He solemnly explained that if we could put volunteer doctors in touch with him, he would arrange for the payment of visas, and provide board and accommodation for up to one month in exchange for work in the clinic and surrounding region.

Taking his business card and making our goodbyes, we headed out on the trail. It was going to be a big day downhill and we still had to face the much famed Ulleri Steps.

With the rain over night, the stone stairs were slick and we needed to be careful any time it became steep. The low, overcast sky did not seem to hold the promise of rain even though the clouds hung heavily. Passing the clinic, I could not see Binu anywhere. I had wanted to say goodbye to her but at least I had her email address and the memory of her bright smile.

Our trail took us through a glistening rain forest alongside the Bhurungdi Khola. Ferns grew out of the sides of trees, hanging mosses dripped water on us as we passed by. The boys were quite chatty and we laughed while bouncing down the stairs. My video camera once again did the rounds as each of them took clips of each other and me picking my way down the rocks. We had become good friends over the last few weeks.

Mid-morning, we stopped for lemon and honey tea at Nangge Thanti (2,430 metres). It was a magnificent view across the valley to the vast rhododendron forests. Sadly we were half a year out on seeing them in full bloom.

From the low cloud overhead we could hear the morning flights to and from Jomsom. The air was fresh, warm and steamy but the likelihood of heavy rain seemed far away.

One of our goals for the day was to descend the Ulleri Steps to the valley below us. Often we thought we had already begun the climb down but the boys kept assuring us that we had some time to go. Our legs had begun to feel the ache from constantly heading down slope. Heading in the other direction uphill were groups of exhausted travellers. I didn't have the heart to tell them that there was more to go before they were done for the day.

At one point, walking through a narrow rock pass with a pretty waterfall, we came across one of the couples we had met on and off over the last couple of weeks. The woman was doubled over suffering from nausea and vomiting. While we suspected food poisoning, we had no medication left that we could spare. Apart from offering sympathy and advice, there was nothing more we could do and we had to leave them to it. Fortunately a group travelling up the trail that we spoke to said that they had some medication and that they would check on the couple when they caught up to them.

Lunch was taken at Ban Thanti (2,210 metres) not far from the start of the famous Ulleri Steps. From here we could look out over the valley below. Staff at the lodge where we stopped were madly attempting to finish building a new dining room. Mike stopped and chatted to them about their construction techniques while we waited for our meals.

Outside, the boys soaked up some sunshine while Dorje had appropriated a guitar from somewhere and strummed a quiet tune to himself. Sneakily we managed to get a short snippet of video as he was singing. Sandra and Mike enjoyed a spicy daal bhaat and masala tea.

Image: Mike Evans

223

We began the climb down the Ulleri Steps. These famous, well-constructed steps number nearly 3,300 hand-laid stone. At times steep, we passed home after home beside the path. Local kids bounced past us laughing and giggling. They seemed more like mountain goats than children the way they could handle the incline. While being afforded some spectacular views, it was somewhat dangerous to take your eyes off your feet when moving. Vertigo was a constant risk.

Near a tree growing beside the path, some of the stones had fallen away in a small landslip. Someone had retrieved a few of the stones and built a narrow trail on the opposite side of the tree. It was more a pony trail than a formal path and we crossed it quickly in case the tree decided to give way.

For a while, I walked with Stewart from Canada who was trekking solo without a guide. He was entertaining me with his stories of India until he was waylaid by a large group of children demanding pens, 'sweets' and stickers.

At the bottom of the stairs we stopped at Tikkedhungga (1,540 metres) where we enjoyed some unsweetened, lumpy buffalo yoghurt. Sandra thought it was delicious. Nearby, a rowdy game was going on. While our thighs and knees complained of the steep descent, the boys had disappeared into the hotel building. It quickly became apparent that they had found a game of 'Spit' based on the shouting, laughing and table slapping from the room above us.

Such was the interest shown in this game, it had travelled down the trail ahead of us being taught from memory alone. The porters had taken to it with cries of glee. It was going to take some time to drag them away so we indulged in another glass of yoghurt.

Stewart eventually caught up to us but didn't stop. He stated he was heading for Lumle where he hoped to catch the last bus of the day. With a decided limp, we considered it unlikely he would get there in time as the last bus was at 17:00, meaning he had to cover that ground in three hours.

Much to our surprise, bouncing down the steps swinging his walking stick with a huge grin on his face, came Captain Pun looking fresh as a daisy. We had departed at about 08:30 this morning and had been on the trail for five and a half hours. He had departed at 11:30 and had already caught up to us. Captain Pun was heading for the same bus at Lumle. Once a Ghurkha, always a Ghurkha, we had no doubt he would make it with time to spare. He was on his way to Pokhara for the festival

It was decided we still had more walking to do for the day and after chiselling the boys away from the card games, we walked on for a short while longer along a gently rolling path before stopping at Hile (1,430 metres). Our accommodation was at the two-storey Sushma Lodge and Restaurant. Brilliantly white-washed, the trims were all in glossy brown and sky blue. On the first floor balcony handrail, lines of corn were hung to dry. On either end wall just underneath the roof line were hung logs which served as beehives. On the floor in the dining room at the back was a small hand-powered mill for grinding maize.

In the space under the building, a man sat turning a butter churn with a long rope. He obviously thought we were a bit strange taking photos and video of this obviously boring and mundane task.

Our evening meal was cooked by the daughter of the household who beamed charmingly when we exclaimed how good the food was.

Sandra enjoyed the vegetable moussaka. It seemed to have a potato base and had yak cheese on top.

However it was a somewhat sombre mood since we all knew our adventure was coming to an end. For the first time in nearly three weeks, a newspaper was found sitting on the table which I think I read from front to back... even the advertisements in Devangari script. A pretty, lacy green moth hung upside down from the rafter above our table.

As full dark descended, tiny pin-pricks of light could be seen from the assorted farms and towns around the valley. Sounds of life drifted on the breeze from all around; a baby crying, children laughing, the click of food ware.

Utterly exhausted, we retired for our final night, each with our own rooms since no-one else was booked in. A rain shower began to fall as I dozed off.

Chapter 11 - The end is in sight

"Not all those who wander are lost." — *J.R.R. Tolkien, the Fellowship of the Ring*

Ah the joy of waking up in a new place even when it is your last day there. The final day of our trek! Eventually the rain passed over night and morning dawned with patchy cloud. Cool green surrounds began to warm as the sun broke through.

We enjoyed a varied breakfast, and Sandra braved the muesli with fruit and buffalo curd and coffee with buffalo milk.

Gathering outside the front of the building that morning, several local families were lined up along the seats outside the front of the hotel. We exchanged pleasantries whilst various members of our group gathered their belongings, adjusted pack straps on our ever narrowing waist lines and took a few pictures as lasting reminders of this final stop on the trail.

As I was wandering around filming some of the plants that grew in such profusion, plants that would normally be just pot plants at home, a passing donkey train jingle-jangled its way past; the brassy bells clanging in a cacophony of sounds.

Behind them, bouncing his way down the stairs we had come the afternoon before was the young porter that Mike had spoken to in Ghorepani. As he spotted our group, and in particular Mike, his face broke out into a huge grin. Diving over to Mike, he shook hands vigorously. The tiny Nepali hand disappearing into Mike's much larger one. It seemed that he had elected to leave his clients behind as they had been less than caring about his welfare. From the worry we had seen two days ago, he now seemed to have shed that burden as well, standing tall and proud.

During the day as we walked, our conversation had become as relaxed as the gentle slopes of the trail in front of us. When we had started, the two groups, porters and trekkers, had been going through that awkward phase of meeting new people for the first time. Now as we began to wind up our journey, the banter was faster, easier, more convivial. The boys even took turns using my video camera to catch their own personal perspective on our journey.

We shared personal histories, now that we had to concentrate less on where our feet needed to go. The stone paving was almost completely flat. We talked about our families, other climbs and treks, and even compared our countries. While Dorje had quickly become a friend, the others had been slower at bonding. Perhaps it was due to a lack of confidence in their English and our almost non-existent Nepali. Whatever the reason, they were now more inclined to talk and joke at our (or maybe just my) expense. Even shy Purna told me of his wife and children.

With the sounds of the river growing ever stronger, the path began to follow the meandering water stream. Above us on the steep green slopes, terraces had been cut into the hillsides. Not one square metre had been wasted in an effort to grow food and house livestock; something we had noticed on the entire journey.

Speaking of livestock, we began to see more and more mobs of goats being moved down trail while individual goats could be seen tethered at many houses. These goats often had a coloured marking on one or both horns indicating that they were to be sacrificed in the coming Hindu festival of Dashain. An idea that Dorje explained was abhorrent to Buddhists since it involved the taking of lives. It was the only time I saw a major difference of opinion between Hindus and Buddhists. The boys explained that while some Buddhists eat meat, often Hindus are employed as the butchers in a village.

At one guesthouse where we stopped for some tea, the entire family was involved in the process of butchering a freshly killed goat. Even the toddler was helping as they cleaned and washed the intestines for making sausage casing. Meanwhile a couple of the men were using khukuri knives to efficiently mince the meat and organs along with green herbs for the filling. Mike coaxed the grandmother of the family to have her picture taken by flattering her outrageously, which brought peals of laughter from her. As I filmed, Dhan stepped in and held up the goat head for my camera. Something I was reasonably certain my parents would not have wanted to see. His cheeky grin showed that they were still trying to find things to shock me. Margaret made use of the squat toilet while here, but horror of horrors her sunglasses fell into the toilet! They were delicately retrieved and washed albeit in cold water.

Image: Mike Evans

The trail still beckoned us and so with farewells to the entire family, we carried on down the trail.

When I had first begun this journey, my fear of heights had been extremely strong. Kanchha in particular liked to wait until I was well onto a suspension bridge before jumping up and down a few times to watch me grab hold of the sides. Now my fears were well and truly controlled. As we began to cross the last bridge, Kanchha was in for a rude surprise. As he reached the middle of the bridge, I ran onto it as heavily as I could. With the cheeky grin now mine, I watched as he quickly grabbed a side and turned round to see me bearing down on him. We both laughed and gingerly walked off the now swaying bridge. The others were left to wait for it to stabilise.

As we walked alongside the now constant river, we encountered another goat herder feverishly counting and recounting his goats. We questioned him over the sound of the river and he yelled back that he was one short. At this time of the year, the price of goats was very high and it was worth a lot of money to him at the markets. Fortunately we had seen the goat just back up the track munching on some succulent green foliage. With much smiling and waving of hands, he left the rest of the flock to go after the recalcitrant goat.

In the cool forests we eventually stopped for ginger tea and banana pancakes at a prosperous looking lodge beside a lovely looking waterfall on the outskirts of Birethanti (1,050 metres).

After a short stop, we shouldered packs once again. The whole town showed evidence of the money associated with trekkers. The paths were not only paved but level. Shops showed the range of knock-off clothing and packs, boots and coats.

We crossed a solid built bridge and entered the poorer looking village of Nayapul. The paving was gone and we were walking on dirt again, dodging puddles. Dorje made the final stop at the official check point so that our permits could be recorded for the last time.

I remember a young American boy wandering down the street loudly asking his mother where the trash can was. At the time I thought it was nice that he would be trying to be clean however I guessed he would quickly learn that, in most cases, rubbish is just dumped on the trail or into the river.

While Dorje finished up the paperwork, the rest of the boys took us further on to our final stop. Walking beside the river, we passed a local butcher 'shop.' Well I use the term advisedly since the 'shop' was actually just the carcasses splayed across the grass in the sun. The workers chopped and hacked at the frames, efficiently turning water buffalo into cuts of meat ready for sale.

After a quick search we found a footbridge across the side stream rather than wade through the river and we popped up onto the road which was full of cars and busses waiting for customers to transport.

We had arrived; the culmination of 18 months training and planning. Our trek had come to a conclusion. Foot in front of foot, we had covered around 210 kilometres, climbed to 5,416 metres, crossed bridges, landslides and an assortment of terrain. All this had taken us just 19 days.

A tear hovered on the edge of my eye while my legs quivered like jelly. Bags and packs dropped to the ground while we took in the final view. Around us drivers quickly descended to try and pick up some work. The boys fended them off while on the other side of the stream, a shrill whistle came from Dorje and Dhan as they jogged to catch up with us.

A variety of buses and cars came and went. Dorje inspected car after car until he was satisfied. Securing the services of two Suzuki Swifts, our bags were once again loaded on to the roofs without being tied down, something that still made me uncomfortable even though we never lost any bags. Splitting up between the cars, Dorje, Margaret, Sandra and I took the first one. Mike, Dhan, Kanchha and Purna took the other. Climbing aboard, we searched vainly for seatbelts but quickly gave it up. Of course they are a rarity and almost never worn even if fitted. With a rumble and a roar, the cars took off along the road to Pokhara. Avoiding the pot holes and weaving around the crumbling edges of the road the cars shared space with buses and trucks traveling in both directions.

With my video camera in hand again, I asked Margaret and Sandra of their thoughts now that the trek was over. The consensus of opinion was sadness to be leaving the trail but joy at the thought of soft beds and hot showers. Turning the camera to Dorje, I was unprepared to his reply. For the last few weeks, we have been teaching him 'ockerisms' (for non-Australian readers, this is a form of English slang specific to Australia). He replied with a laugh, "they stone the flaming crows." Normally this is an epithet of frustration, but with Dorje's slight accent, it caused us to break into fits of giggles. His big grin had us laughing as turned back to enjoy the breeze from window.

However the joy of moving by means other than foot was short lived. After a mere 20 minutes, Mike's car came to an abrupt stop. Catching up to them we pulled over to see what was happening. Gathered around the front left wheel all the boys were squatting with the driver. Off came the wheel and assorted hands poked around inside the wheel arch. Mike's considered opinion was that the brake had locked up and would not release. We stretched our legs and watched the hodgepodge of vehicles passing us by. A bus wheezed its way up the hill, a goat sitting proudly on the roof. Two road workers tirelessly patched the edges of the road. Between them they had a shovel, a mattock and even one safety vest. Shyly they grinned at me filming their work.

After 20 minutes of struggling with the problem, Dorje flagged down an empty car and we switched vehicles. Leaving the hapless driver to struggle with the fault, we headed on our way along the winding roads. For the first time in many weeks we hit 80 kilometres per hour, a scary prospect without seatbelts. Mike's car hit 95 as they overtook us on a straight stretch of road. We climbed up the winding roads before cresting a saddle pass and looked down on the city of Pokhara (820 metres) sitting under a veil of haze. Dropping down into the valley, we hit well made highways and our pace remained constant. That is until we encountered mobs of goats being herded towards the markets.

Hitting the outskirts of the city, our travels stalled as we encountered huge crowds of revellers. Everyone seemed to be on foot as they bought goods for the upcoming religious holidays. After having driven so fast for the first time in ages, it took an hour to cross town to our accommodation. Again cars seemed to create whole new lanes for traffic flow. A taxi attempted to merge with our lane. In its back seat sat two goats. Pedestrians walking between the cars would occasionally reach in the window and touch them on the head.

After three weeks of peace and quiet, the sound was almost deafening. In all directions people were dressed in bright colours. The mood was festive in the hot, dry, dusty air. Loud music played from nearby shop fronts. Children ran through the slow moving traffic. Even amid this chaos, the traffic would divert around cows chewing their cud in the middle of the roads.

The driver's frustration eventually showed and he cut down some back roads. The traffic was much calmer away from the main roads. Our destination was the tourist suburb of Lakeside. After cutting to and fro, we eventually were deposited on a dirt back road outside the Hotel Lake Diamond. We were confronted with tall metal gates and a high stone wall. As the second taxi arrived, we were greeted by the smiling hotel owner and his little dogs. Swinging the gates wide for us, he welcomed the tired, and probably smelly, group inside. An oasis garden stretched around the building inside the walls. Leaving the heat of the day as we crossed the beautiful marble portico, the cool foyer was a blessing. The owner, Mankuma, spoke with Dorje before quickly recognising both Mike and Margaret from their previous visits.

Taking the briefest of details, he ushered us up the stairs to the second floor. Unlocking the concertina grill door, we were given exclusive access to our own level. I was shown into my room. A palatial carpeted space with a luxurious queen-sized bed greeted me. Joy of joys, a ceiling fan sat directly over it and in the corner a small TV. Opposite the entry door was a large tiled ensuite with throne-style toilet and shower with hot water.

I quickly divested myself of my grubby clothes and enjoyed my first long hot shower in days. Reaching for my razor, the days of facial growth were scraped away. Aching legs and feet began to relax and I suddenly began to realise how smelly the days on the trail had made me.

As I towelled myself dry, the comfort of the bed beckoned me but I resisted as I could hear the others passing my room for the balcony. I dressed and wandered out to join everyone else, a fresh pot of tea and cups for everyone were waiting. Sandra was updating her diary.

From the balcony, we had views across Phewa Tal to the west and north to the peaks like Machhapuchhare also known as 'Fish Tail'. The weather was now hot and exceptionally muggy; more coastal tropical than a lake side at the top of the sub-continent. Feeling much refreshed, the remaining members of the Thorung Five sat down to tote up our self-imposed fines. The value in rupee turned out to be quite decent, suitable enough for the boys to be able to buy a decent meal that evening. We discussed our plans to get custom embroidered t-shirts of the trip made up by one of the many stores down on the main shopping strip. Having noted that a laundry service was on offer to hotel guests, I elected to use it for the minimal fee of NPR160 so that I would have very little to clean up back at home. As Sandra said, "What a luxury."

Finding energy from somewhere, we wandered down the side road to the shops. Walking in either direction we were able to enjoy some unhurried window shopping. Mike and Margaret wanted to stop in on a camping supplies store belonging to someone they had made friends with on their last visit. During our wanderings, we began running into various groups from our weeks on the trail. The Spanish brothers, some of the Israeli group, the British boys on gap year, even the two lovely oncology nurses from New Zealand. We would briefly discuss our choices for accommodation, good restaurants and bad, and even their preferred night clubs though we had no plans to visit them.

After some searching, we finally found a t-shirt shop that would suit our purposes. We haggled over prices and selected five shirts. The price was reasonable coming in at $AU9.00 per shirt embroidered. It was agreed we would pick them up at lunch time the next day. All the work was going to be done by eye using a standard sewing machine.

With the shopping done, we returned to the hotel and the great views from the balcony. Eventually the boys joined us and they were a much different group. La Har, who lives in Pokhara, put in an appearance. Showered, shaved and dressed in their fine clothes, it was hard to imagine they were the same hard working porters we had shared the trail with. Mike and Margaret led the speeches, thanking them for their hard work. Sandra put out the last of her 'children's bounty' and offered the boys choices of stickers, pencils and balloons for their kids.

Our self-imposed fines for leaving items behind had totalled a sizeable sum. For every forgotten item, we had to stump up 100 rupee. Not one of us had remembered to collect all our items but the eagle eyes of the boys had located about 99% of them. The collected fines were turned over to the care of Dorje to pay for their meal that night. Apparently a rare treat of pork was going to be on the menu.

Dorje spoke on behalf of the group; hoping that we had enjoyed ourselves and offering a heartfelt wish that we would return to Nepal. There was no doubt in our minds we would do just that. Already an idea was forming in my mind about a return visit.

There was one drawback that he had to alert us to. A small problem had occurred with booking our return flight to Kathmandu. Instead of having all day to wander Pokhara the next day, we were now flying out early in the morning. An inconvenience at most, we would have to try and get our shirts first thing in the morning.

In the discrete manner of the Nepali, we each took our porters aside where personal thankyous were given along with a cash bonus to supplement wages. Nothing was said by the porters and no reply was expected. This is a very personal thing that is not discussed with the Nepalese but you know that they appreciate the offer. Much to my embarrassment, I did not have enough Nepali rupees. I think Dorje may have thought less of me at that moment but I had not been near an ATM in weeks. It was something I intended to fix as soon as we headed out for an evening meal. I would not have my new friend feeling dishonoured any longer than I could help.

This was the last time of this journey we would see Purna and La Har. They would remain and pick up new trekkers. Kanchha and Dhan we would see in Kathmandu although they were returning by bus. We hugged good-bye and with one or two tears, bid them farewell. Hopefully next time we returned we would catch up again.

We strolled down the laneway and popped out on to Baidam Road. This is most definitely the party district of Lakeside. Bars, clubs, restaurants, shops all packed in side-by-side. For those from Australia, Lakeside is a little bit like Surfers Paradise but much more intimate, with better style and much   better prices.

Wandering along the road to find a restaurant, we popped in to the t-shirt shop and explained the change in pick up time. To our surprise, the gentleman at the sewing machine asked us to check in once we had finished our meal. He planned on completing the job by that time even though he had not yet started. Thanking him, we carried on down the road nodding to our various trail companions as they sorted out the evening's meal.

Selecting a pleasant looking restaurant, we chose a range of western dishes to dine on. Mike and I sipped on local beer while we waited for the food to arrive. I remember getting a chicken dish which was both generous and delicious. Sandra had lemon chicken, mash and vegetables. There was a dessert in there somewhere and by the time we were finished, I was fuller than I had been in a long time. Several bottles of beer had been consumed and we were feeling very relaxed. We laughed and chatted about our experiences.

It soon came time to head back to the hotel although there was a bit of shopping to do on the way. Stopping in at the t-shirt shop, as promised, all five shirts were ready for pickup. At home this might not be considered an important fact but given this had all been done by hand without templates in less than two hours, it was quite an achievement. Only tailors chalk and a good eye had been used to replicate the shirts. Packing them into our bags, we perused the other shops. I had an order for a doll in traditional dress from a friend at home. Wandering from one shop to the next, I finally found some marionettes in assorted clothing styles. A bit of haggling and chatting with the owner, I finally managed to pick them up for 'evening price' paying only a couple of hundred rupees for two of them. For the trip home, I also picked up a book on the history of the Ghurkhas for about 700 rupees.

During the trek, we had discovered that the price of goods varied through the day. A 'morning price' is for a quick sale when you are setting up your shop or stall first thing and don't have time for a full haggle. The 'day price' is the regular price, and the 'evening price' is reduced so a quick sale can be had and people can get home. You were expected to haggle everywhere except if it was at one of the purely tourist supply places that deal almost exclusively with internationals. These prices were fixed.

Walking back up the side road to our accommodation, the sounds of revelry were also completely lost within minutes. Eventually we returned to Hotel Lake Diamond where, exhausted, I was quickly asleep under the rare joy of a ceiling fan.

After weeks of training, the following morning I was awake and up long before the others. Stepping onto the balcony, I tried to film the surrounding peaks but they were lost in the fog and low cloud. The lake was just visible to the west. As we ate our breakfast, my laundry came back. It was still damp but normally it would have had the heat of the day to finish off. At least I would be able to hang it out at the Benchen Vihar guesthouse around lunch time.

Our transport arrived and the bags were once again packed on top without restraints. We said our goodbyes to Kanchha and Dhan before piling into the vehicle. The driver quickly had us at Pokhara Airport which is like many other domestic airports the world over. Clear open spaces were well swept which was good since it was crowded, noisy and already beginning to become hot. Our bags were checked in and we moved up to the rooftop viewing deck to wait the next hour for the flight.

The strongest memory I have is of a sky blue bowl painted with mountains then inverted over the valley. The fog had lifted and all the way around us were hills and the peaks of the Annapurna. Dorje was pointing out the various peaks as I tried to keep up with the video camera.

The sun was already hot but the breeze was cool off the lake. An assortment of light aircraft and para-gliders were landing in tight coordination with commercial flights. From time to time, they would be landing from both ends of the runway at the same time.

Eventually it was time for us to head through to the departure gate. Stepping through the metal detector arch expecting it to be triggered by my hips, I noticed it wasn't even plugged in. I was ushered into a booth where a nice young official politely asked a few questions, checked my bag and gave me a quick pat down.

Our time in the departure lounge was quick and we boarded our small Agni Air flight. The attendant, in a long ankle-length traditional style skirt, invited us on board before passing round a tray with cotton wool balls and lollies on it. The cotton wool was for our ears while the lollies could be sucked to encourage them to pop during the climb to cruising altitude. In the cockpit, the pilot and co-pilot could be seen programming a Garmin GPS unit similar to one used in cars. The blades began to turn over and we prepared to roll onto the taxiway. With a burst of power, we charged down the runway and climbed into the morning sky.

Through the left windows, the peaks of the Annapurna slipped by. The blades of the engine made odd patterns on the screen of my video camera. With a twinge of sadness I noted that our 50 minute flight would complete the loop of the Annapurna Conservation Reserve. I looked with amazement at the ground we had covered during the previous 19 days. Below us the heavily textured landscape slid by. Individual vehicles could be seen winding along the highway.

Before long we flew over the pass and dropped down into the Kathmandu valley. With a sweeping turn we came in to a neat landing on the runway at Tribhuvan Airport before taxiing to the domestic terminal. Quickly disembarking, we gathered our bags and grabbed transport to the monastery. The roads were surprisingly quiet owing to the approaching Hindu festival and in short order we were deposited in the forecourt of the BPD Monastery. Our journey was almost at an end as we climbed to the guesthouse.

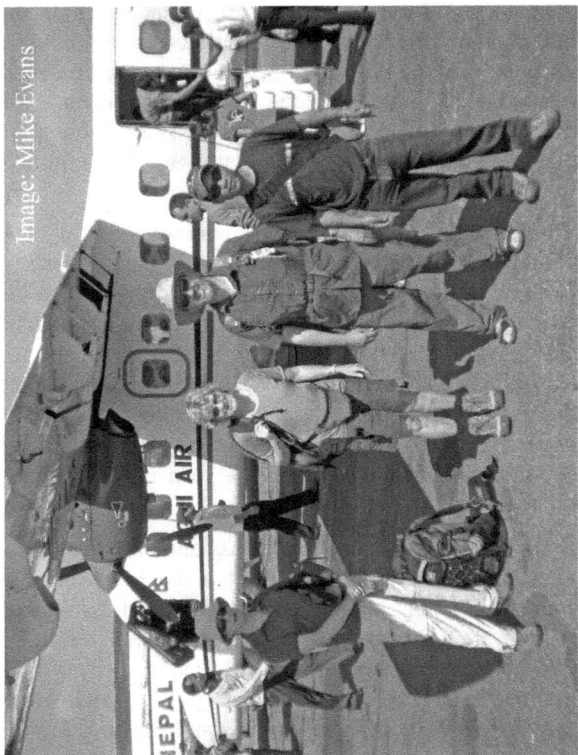

Image: Mike Evans

After an hour or two setting up our rooms again we prepared to head down to Thamel. In those few hours, Mike, Sandra and I went for a walk to buy prayer flags at a local 'tailor' shop. Along the way we saw young children enjoying giant swings, which had been set up for the festival. They were very high and seemed flimsy but everyone was having a grand time.

With regret, I took back my damaged day pack to the shop where they replaced it without argument. The rented sleeping bags were returned and paid for. With a little light shopping under our belt, we had an early dinner at our favourite restaurant - Weizen Bakery off J.P. Road. Sandra remembers having chicken sizzler on a real sizzling plate, chips and vegetables and another banana lassi. Mike and I tried the chicken tandoori. It came with a small bowl containing a green sauce. Feeling game, I sampled a bit and found it to be very hot. Dipping pieces of the chicken into it, the sauce actually began to compliment the yoghurt coating. I demolished the whole bowl (my mouth was burning) and yet Mike decided against having too much, stating it was "too hot."

When the waiters came to remove our plates, I asked what the sauce was. With a raised eyebrow, he looked at me straight-faced and said it was parsley sauce. "Did it contain chilli?" I asked. "A little," was his reply as his face broke into a grin. When I stated that it was delicious, his grin became broader. It would take me another two years before I found a recipe that matched its taste and heat.

As the light began to fail, we decided to forego a taxi back to the monastery. This was an interesting journey as about 15 minutes in, our area of the city lost power so everything was being done by vehicle headlight. There were the odd homes that had solar charged lights but mostly the light was very dim.

The path to and from Thamel was becoming very familiar. Sandra and I were well in front of the others in the dark as we passed the police post at the foot of Swayambhunath. As we walked past, a voice from behind us in the dark called out "hello" and we spun around to see an off-duty policeman following us. It turned out he was going our way and had decided to walk with us to practise his English while providing a little protection. He seemed very surprised when we explained how much we loved his country. Asking lots of questions about Australia, he expressed an interest in visiting one day but had difficulty understanding why we would come to Nepal. We described the trek we had done and then it became clearer to him. He thought we were in love with the smelly, over-crowded city. I didn't have the heart to explain to him I loved the city too.

Parting company near the monastery, we headed for bed, our journey almost over. One more day and we would be heading home. As my eyes closed, my mind had firmly clamped on one idea. I would be back.

Epilogue

"Why do you go away? So that you can come back. So that you can see the place you came from with new eyes and extra colors. And the people there see you differently, too. Coming back to where you started is not the same as never leaving." — Terry Pratchett, A Hat Full of Sky

Here my diary ends. I had reached a point where I did not want to write any more. The memories, the blog, the pictures and video are what I have left of this special time.

We did spend the next day at Bhaktapur after struggling to find the NPR1,500 in our now vastly drained purses. Wandering the broad avenues, we enjoyed the views of the 55 Window Palace amongst other wonders. Visiting a Thanka School, we viewed a range of paintings and I even allowed myself to be talked into parting with some substantial Australian dollars for a mid-range piece for Kim. Mike and I haggled with a young lad for a painted wooden toy truck. With much smiling and laughing, we settled on a price. Why a truck, you may ask? Every truck we had seen had positive and uplifting messages written on their backs. This toy had our favourite message; 'Horn Please.' It sits on a special shelf at home as a reminder, bringing a sly smile to my lips even now.

The final day dawned and we enjoyed breakfast on the lawn of the guesthouse. Mangal's wife dropped by for a visit and gave us each a silk scarf or katas, Tibetan symbols of greeting or on departure, and some incense sticks before heading off to work. We spent a bit of time with the friendly monks who had looked after us and the possessions we did not carry on the trek. Dorje soon arrived with Kanchha after arranging for our taxi to the airport. We were honoured with more silk scarves by the boys. Taking that last walk out of the monastery, we watched the young monks playing an impromptu game of soccer using a stone. Waving good bye and saying our Namastes, we headed across the forecourt with bags in tow.

The journey was slow in the traffic but we still arrived with plenty of time to spare. Dorje and Kanchha had to leave us at the front door as they were not permitted to enter the building without tickets. Hugging them tightly, I promised them that I would be back within a couple years. My throat was tight as we waved goodbye and turned to enter the terminal.

We left our friends behind as we began the extended trip home. Not quite tears but it was really hard to leave this beautiful, smelly, overcrowded, visually exciting place.

Entering the terminal, checking bags, clearing customs, all this had become pretty standard. We even managed to secure extra leg room on both segments of our homeward journey, but how is our little secret. Right, down to the sounds of the metal detector's beeeeeepppp... Here we go again. In the departure lounge, a cry of "Kia Ora" had me turning to be reunited with the two oncology nurses from New Zealand. We were sharing the flight to Singapore before separating to our final destinations.

Our pilot, rough during take-off, gave us one courtesy. He came on the over-head speaker and advised us we would be flying north before circling to the right around Mount Everest before heading to Singapore. Sadly, despite his best efforts however, we still did not get to see this magnificent peak as it was completely shrouded in clouds. So with some disappointment, we settled back into our seats for the remainder of the flight.

Many hours later we eventually disembarked in Australia. I was by now struggling to hold my trousers up, having lost so much weight in the preceding weeks. My parents met me at the airport and there were hugs, greetings and introductions all round.

Over the next few weeks I settled back into regular life. But I noticed an interesting effect or two of my travels. Yes, my big toe nail did eventually fall off as expected after the incident with the water bottle. But I also noted a 'famine' ripple on all my nails. It would take over six months before it eventually grew out but it was there all the same.

The idea that had come to me towards the end of the trek would appear in my thoughts over the coming years. Many of us wanted to help Dorje's home village to get their health post up and running. But getting up-to-date information from there was proving cumbersome and difficult. Since I had wanted to return to Nepal, I planned to visit his home and meet people. It would give me a chance to meet locals who were not directly involved in the tourism industry and I could still find the information required to help support the project.

In 2011 I returned with Mike, Sandra and my friend Faye and we spoke with the lovely people of Pattale. It is from that visit that I was encouraged to write this book. And the health post? Well that went forward and is running to this day. A percentage of the sales of this book will go to support that work.

My memory of the journey has not been perfect and at the same time, I have remembered other things that I had not committed to writing. Photos have drawn a wry smile from me. Events have been relived with the members of the Thorung Five. All of this will be with me for the rest of my life.

I had conquered my fears, climbed higher than anyone else in my family and made firm friends with a whole new group of people. Hopefully this will inspire you to visit somewhere you have never been.

Thank you for travelling with me on this journey.

Namaste to you all

Ian

Postscript:

As of December 2012, the road to Manang has been opened. Dorje has shown me photos of motorbikes on the same road where only foot traffic or horses would have been able to reach when we were there in 2009.

Appendix

The day by day accounts of our travel in Nepal can be found at:

http://danthonia.wordpress.com/

Author's note: Owing to the general exhaustion and delays between functioning internet, some items appear out of sequence or on the wrong days while completing the blog. Hey! I was tired. :-)

Dorje Tamang - Nepalonfoot

Trekking for small groups and individuals
http://www.nepalonfoot.com/
Pattale Health Project
http://www.pattalecommunityhealth.org/

Pattale Health Trust - Trustees

Recipes

Let's talk about just a few recipes related to the food that we consumed while in Nepal. These are purely my interpretations of the foods we tried and are not necessarily true representations. The tastes, however, are definitely authentic to my memory.

Ginger-lemon-honey drink

What a refreshing hot drink to have on a hot day. In my blog, I noticed that I had omitted the most important ingredient. Tea! Don't make that mistake.

Boil your kettle of water.
Into a large tea pot, put two tea bags, two and a half cm (one inch) of bruised or julienned ginger and a generous teaspoon per person of strong honey.
Pour over the boiling water and allow the mix to steep for about 5 minutes.
Serve by straining the mix.

Banana Lassi

This refreshing drink can be made thick or thin. Chilled and thick, it can even be used as a replacement for custard over other fruit. Feel free to experiment with different flavours.

- 2 cups of natural or Greek yoghurt
- 2 cups of ice
- 1/3 cup of raw sugar (try to avoid processed sugar, you'll thank me)
- 2 bananas

- 1 teaspoon ground cinnamon
- 1/8 teaspoon of ground cardamom
- Optional extras:
- 2 cups of milk (for a thinner version)
- Finely chopped ginger (can be added for a little more zing!)
- Mild honey can be substituted for the sugar

Put all ingredients into a blender, processing until it is smooth.

Serve straight away in tall glasses under shade with good friends on a hot day.

Green Sauce

This is great with seafood or for dipping tandoori chicken into. Careful, it will bite but it complements the yoghurt coating on the chicken.

- 3 green chillies – jalapeno or similar would be fine
- 1 ½ cups of firmly packed parsley
- 2-3 big cloves of garlic
- 2-3 anchovies fillets
- Olive oil
- Juice of ½ a lemon or lime

If you don't want so much heat, de-seed the chilli. Make sure you wear gloves or wash your hands before touching ANYTHING else.

Roughly chop and place the chillies and parsley in a mortar with the garlic and anchovies.

Pound the mix well with the pestle until it forms a combined mash.

Add a little of the oil and continue pounding until it begins to make a paste.

Continue adding the oil and stir with the pestle until everything is well mixed.

Add the lemon or lime juice to taste.

MoMos

These are my favourite dish and I will always order them at least once every few days. The fillings can vary widely but the flavours are enjoyable no matter what.

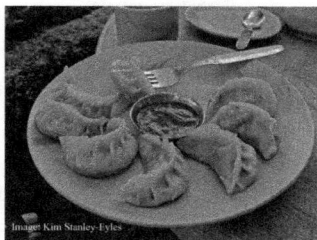
Image: Kim Stanley-Eyles

- Flour
- Water
- 1 onion
- 2 cloves garlic
- Finely chopped ginger
- Shredded cabbage
- 1 cup of chopped spinach

- Julienned carrot
- Boiled and chopped potato
- 1½ ground coriander seeds
- Cumin, cayenne, turmeric, pepper and salt

Mix the flour and water together to make a smooth dough. (Commercial spring roll or gyoza wrappers may be substituted to save time.)

Roll it up then allow it to rest.

Heat oil in a pan and cook off the onion and garlic until soft.

Add the remaining spices and stir to release the flavours.

Stir in the vegetables until the mixture begins to dry up.

Portion off the dough and roll the portions into flat discs approximately 7 centimetres wide.

Cool the filling before spooning amounts onto each disc.

Fold together the edges and crimp them so the momo is completely sealed.

Keep the completed momos moist whilst filling the remaining ones.

Steam the dumplings for approximately 10 minutes or until the dough is translucent.

Serve them immediately with an assortment pickles for dipping.

Garlic Soup (thanks to Jyoti Pathak for sourcing this recipe)

- 1 tablespoon full scoop butter
- 1 cup of peeled and smashed garlic
- 2 tablespoon full of white flour (maida)
- Some salt and pepper

Heat the butter but don't let it get black.
Brown the garlic until you get a nice smell (should not be too dark).
Fry the maida and keep stirring fast till it browns.
Then pour 3-4 cups of water and boil till it thickens.
Put salt and garnish with freshly milled pepper (use pepper grinder).
My trials have shown that it could have a 'fuller' flavour if a homemade stock is used instead of water.

Glossary

Here you will find an assortment of words and the approximate translation. I won't claim that the translation is 100% correct but I have done the best I could in the circumstances. This isn't meant to be comprehensive, just a few of the words in the text. If there are any errors you note, please contact me and I will arrange for them to be incorporated in later editions.

ACAP	Annapurna Conservation Area Project aims to ensure sustainable tourism whilst minimising environmental damage to this sensitive, remote area.
Bisari Bisari	Literally means slowly slowly and refers to some taking things easy to ensure that can complete their movement, usually from place to place.
Bush Bashing	Australian colloquialism meaning to push through dense vegetation.
Chiko Roll	A large Australian variant of the spring roll filled with minced pork and vegetables before being wrapped in a thick pastry-type casing before being deep fried.
Danyabad	Thank you
Daal bhaat	A traditional dish of rice and soupy lentils served with a series of pickles ranging from mild to

	extremely spicy.
Ghar	House
Khola	Small river
Lassi	A yoghurt based drink often made with fruit and spices such as cardamom
Marg/Marga	Road
Momo	A delicious form of steamed or fried dumping filled with meat and vegetables
Nadi	River
Namaskar	The formal version of hello or goodbye. It means that you recognise the spirit within the other person. The palms of both hands are placed together under the chin with the fingers pointed straight up.
Namaste	The informal version that is not necessarily performed with palms together under the chin
Pokhari	Meaning pond, lake or reservoir
Ramro	Means good or beautiful. Repeated several times with a laugh means you are often doing something really well such as a foreigner attempting to speak Nepali.
Rajpath	Roughly translates as Royal Path or, I presume, royal highway as these were often major roads stretching across the country.
Sathi/saathi	Friend
Tal	Lake

What readers are saying about
'A Little Bit Up: Meandering in Nepal'

"Three chapters in and I think it's going to be a late night. This is a sensational read." – **Cameron**

"I have for some years assumed that due to my health I would have neither the ability nor the privilege of travelling to Nepal. How wrong I was. Ian Stanley Eyles' book 'A little bit up – Meandering in Nepal' has enabled me to do it.

His beautifully detailed and sensitively written descriptions of the people, the journey, the food, the culture and the utterly breathtaking landscapes, have successfully taken me on all the 'little bit ups' and the 'little bit downs' of the trek around the Annapurna Ranges.

I fortunately was able to complete this journey from the comfort of my own lounge room but Ian's simple, yet clever writing style managed to make me believe that I was short of breath and suffering from altitude sickness, that I was right there patting a Tibetan Mastiff and that I could actually taste the cool and refreshing Lassi.

A wonderful read, a spectacular journey and a fantastic book that provides valuable information to both the armchair and real world traveller.

Thank you for taking me on the journey with you Ian." – **Caroline**

"Each page is making me more and more eager to go and do it for myself. ...it is very inspiring." – **Katelyn**

"An absolutely beautifully written book that I thoroughly enjoyed. Your descriptions of your trip made me feel like I was there trekking right beside you! I felt every ache and pain, I felt the altitude sickness, but I also felt the utter joy you felt at the beautiful scenery you experienced and also the grand accomplishment you achieved! You have a gift for writing!" — **Eva**

Also in print by INK Publications

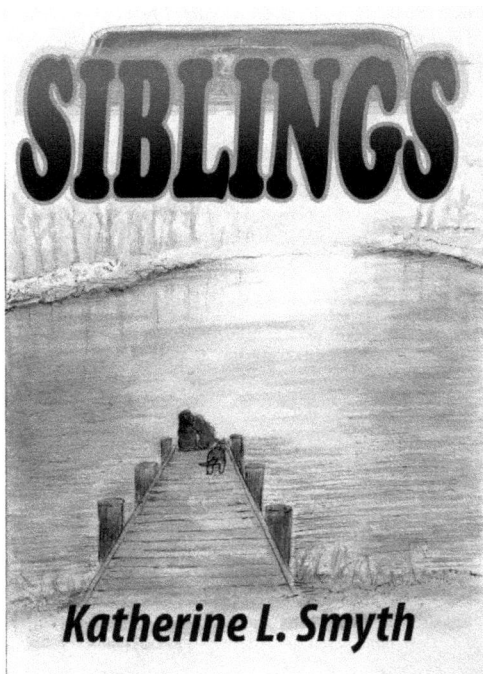

When tragedy strikes on an Australian coastal road, orphaned twins Jared and Asha are thrust into a new way of life in America with family they've never even met.

Sometimes humorous, sometimes haunting, *Siblings* is a vignetted journey through candid snapshots and remembered moments of Asha's life.

Siblings is an engaging tale that touches on the loss of childhood innocence, of coping with grief and struggling through the adversities of being a teenager, and ultimately it is a reminder of the rewards that await perseverance, in life and in love.

www.ingramcontent.com/pod-product-compliance
Lightning Source LLC
Chambersburg PA
CBHW070345090426
42733CB00009B/1291